More than Ghosts: A Guide to Working Residential Cases in the Paranormal Field

ALEX MATSUO

Foreword by Bill Wilkens, Jr.

Edited by Jonda Matsuo and Lorelei Mellon

Cover Design by ilovemycover.com

ISBN: 1495948587
ISBN-13: 978-1495948589

DEDICATION

This book is dedicated to anyone who is trying to find the answers to the unknown. Whether you're a scientist, a psychic, a researcher, or a hunter, we are all still seeking answers and finding that undeniable proof of the afterlife. This book is dedicated to the ones who spend the long nights in the dark, who host the podcasts, who write the articles, and who do the lectures so that we can all learn more. Keep studying, keep investigating!

TABLE OF CONTENTS

ACKNOWLEDGMENTS

I would like to thank my team, the Association of Paranormal Study, for not only being a part of my life, but also keeping me on my toes in this research field. Thank you to Jay, David, Amy, Beverly, Maeve, Beth, Bryan, Lina, Nick, Xavier, Shannon, Flo, Michael, "D", Hearst, and Cheri, for all that you have done and contributed to my paranormal research. Thank you for taking the long road trips so that a family can sleep peacefully at night. Thank you for the late night evidence reviews so that we could take a step closer to finding out if we indeed survive death. Thank you for agreeing and disagreeing with me. Most of all, thank you for being present and loving.

Also, many thanks to Bill Wilkens of ParanormalSocieties.com for his willingness to contribute to this book. Thank you, Bill, for all that you have done for the paranormal community!

FOREWORD

The field of paranormal investigation has grown dramatically since the beginning of the 21st century. The popularity of television shows that focused on the topic spawned a whole new generation of paranormal investigators. Many of those investigators adopted the field as a hobby, while others were able to dedicate their focus to investigation and research full time.

Normally such exposure and increased involvement would be beneficial for the growth of a particular field of research. By and large it has been positive overall, but paranormal research is quite different from any other field of scientific research. There have been no formal schooling or accredited degree programs that focus on the topic, and there are no licensing requirements, certifications, regulations, or governmental oversight (thankfully, I might add).

With that being the case, how would someone go about learning the right and wrong way to research the paranormal? How would you go about properly conducting an investigation? What elements would a proper investigation even entail? Of course there are books and articles on the internet that outline much of that information, but who can you believe? Who do you trust?

Clearly, there is a lot of uncertainty and lack of direction. Many would be investigators enter the field with the best of intentions, but soon grow frustrated with their inability to conclusively find or identify what it is that they're seeking. Others enter the field for entertainment value only, and don't understand the risks involved with pursuing something that can at times be malevolent or potentially harmful.

The most concerning thing that I have found is that many investigators do not know how to properly handle a residential case, or a case that involves an actual client who needs help, but yet they try to take on these cases anyway. It is very different investigating a home where a family or individual actively lives, versus investigating an uninhabited location. People's lives are in turmoil, their performance at work is suffering, their children are scared and are not sleeping at night, etc. It's not fun for them, it's not a game, and they need legitimate help. They can't afford to have someone come in who may potentially make things worse, or someone that is unreliable or unwilling give it their best effort.

Handling residential, or client, cases can be extraordinarily complex and sensitive. There are many factors to take into account when handling a residential case, and investigators need to be well rounded and able to juggle the various issues that may come into play. Investigators especially need to know how to handle clients whose problems are medical or psychological in nature, and not paranormal. If you are not a licensed medical professional, then you should not be making diagnoses of someone's physical or mental state. Doing so can potentially expose you to legal ramifications in the future. There have already been instances of lawsuits being levied against paranormal teams for causing "emotional distress" due to remarks made about a client's state of mind.

It's extremely important to be knowledgeable about the paranormal, but it is equally important to have good people skills as well. Harmful spirits can feed off of fear and negative energy, so a good team will be able to put their client's minds at ease, relieve their fear, and help to restore a calmer, more confident environment in the home. They might not have done anything to identify or eradicate the phenomena, but sometimes just changing the attitude and mindset of those that are affected can make a big difference. They should not do anything that would increase the stress or anxiety level of those that are being affected.

During my time involved with the paranormal, I have handled thousands of cases and have worked with thousands of paranormal investigators and teams. I have seen approaches that work and approaches that don't work. I have seen teams that are flawless in their handling of the varying residential cases I have worked with them on, and I have also seen teams that, though good intentioned, were not yet ready to take on a residential case. Unfortunately, some of the outcomes of those cases were disastrous and could have been avoided. The physical and emotional safety of you, your team, and your client are paramount to everything, and no compromises should be made that in any way jeopardize the well-being of all involved.

There is no shame in admitting if you do find yourself in over your head. It happens to the best of teams, but it's only the best teams that are smart enough to admit it and seek additional help. It is a strength, not a weakness, to know your limitations and to work within them.

All clients are different, and all cases are different. Some are far more difficult than others, and only experience will prepare you to handle the more complex cases. However, going into an investigation with a well-rounded, solid foundation of knowledge in the handling of residential cases will help you immensely. If you have not had the benefit of being able to learn from a more experienced group, then this book will be an excellent place to start your education on the way to properly handle residential cases.

-Bill Wilkens, Jr.
Founder and Operator of ParanormalSocieties.com

MORE THAN GHOSTS

INTRODUCTION

When I decided to write this book, I was met with a lot of support and praise. But inside I was terrified. Mainly because I didn't know how the general paranormal community would respond. Who was I to be advising people on how to investigate? I was never on any TV show, I'm not a person of authority. But I was a paranormal investigator who cared and I still do. I care about how the paranormal community is perceived by "normal" people. I care about how residential cases are handled. I care about people and what they think and perhaps this is my Achilles heel.

My first paranormal experiences weren't anything terrifying or dramatic. I was about 8 years old or so and I was laying down in the guest room of my grandparents' house (where I was living at the time) when something whacked me on the forehead. There were no shelves above me, it was impossible that anything fell off and magically hit me on the head. Comparatively looking back, it's a rather boring experience. But it was the first experience that caught my attention. It was my "uh oh" moment so to speak. Ironically enough, my mom would make this room my bedroom several years later. Unfortunately my next paranormal experience in that room was during my senior year of high school and it wasn't positive.

Now, let's pause here. I'm not implying that this "not-so-positive" experience was evil or demonic, it just wasn't positive. Maybe I misinterpreted a communication attempt or something was attached to me, who knows. This is a subject that I will address later on in the book when it comes to diagnosing cases and deciding on a plan of action if you think there is an evil presence about. But as a preview, know that inhuman doesn't always mean evil.

Between my two experiences in that room and experiences sprinkled in here and there in relatives' houses around the country, it was enough to pique my interest in the paranormal. Enough so that I would go to the library often to read books by Dr. Hans Holzer and any book about the weird and the unknown that I could get my hands on. I would never take these books home because my mother was dead set against having anything related to the occult in the house. I had to beg or go to a friend's house if I wanted to watch anything remotely dark or potentially scary on television.

I suppose it is also worth mentioning that I was raised in a strict Southern Baptist Christian home in Southern California. I know that the words "Southern Baptist" and "Southern California" shouldn't go together, but it is what it is. Anything that was considered to be related to ghosts, spirits, and the occult was traditionally a no-no in church and at home. When one of my classmates brought a book about Wicca to school, I was immediately interested and wanted to learn more. While certain members of my family always acknowledged the paranormal, you still didn't dare speak about it.

So starting from about 11 years old until I was about 23, I was actively researching the paranormal. When I became a legal adult I started watching paranormal reality shows on television. I was entranced by what I saw and I would even well up with tears when I watched other people experiencing paranormal phenomena like I was. Needless to say (especially because of the fact that I brought up paranormal reality shows) I was a naïve person. Even though I was reading regularly and was aware that there were ghost hunters out there, I didn't even know where to begin when it came to investigating. So like many others, I began to emulate what I saw on television and went out ghost hunting by myself. Big mistake. Nothing serious ever happened to me then, but if I had a time machine, I would go back and smack my teenaged self.

The paranormal took a back seat for a few years while I worked on my master's degree. It wasn't because I didn't care about the paranormal or that I lost interest, I just had other things to do. I was very involved in theatre, and loved it (enough to get a graduate degree in it). It was and still is a major priority in my life.

After I graduated in 2011, the paranormal came back into my life, and in the fall of the same year, I started my team: Association of Paranormal Study. And now I had the free time to actually pursue what I had wanted to do for quite a while: paranormal investigating for people who needed help. But as I dove into the paranormal community, I was quickly smacked in the face with a heavy dose of reality. Which brings us to why I wrote this book.

I started investigating the paranormal because I wanted to help people and give them the assistance that I didn't get when I was growing up. Let's face it; there are people out there who are working residential cases that shouldn't be doing it. For a short period of time I was one of those people, until I took a step back and realized how much I was changing another person's life with my presence in their home or business. Many people get into investigating because they saw something glamorized on television. Unfortunately the entertainment industry has released the hounds on clients who may be getting fed the wrong information, being convinced to go public with their story so the investigator can get their 15 minutes of fame and, worst of all, they are being abandoned by thrill seekers and ghost hunters in a state that is no better, or even worse, than when the team first came onto the case.

This book isn't meant to be preachy. But I will level with you, my dear reader. I don't want to feed you any fluff about how amazing of an investigator I am (because I'm not) or how great my team is. I will be exposing to you my biggest mistakes when I first started my team and the things I shouldn't have done or said. I hope that you will learn from my mistakes as I have learned from them, so that you don't have to deal with the same consequences and subsequent guilt that followed. By reading about how I messed up, I hope you can avoid it. I will also bring up the mistakes of others for the purposes of helping you avoid those mistakes as well and help you see the warning signs of potentially negative situations.

But I'm also going to be very direct and strongly express my opinions on how residential cases should be handled, and I will talk about other teams and investigators whose behavior I observed and methods that I disagreed with. Of course most of the names and teams mentioned will have their identities protected so that their reputations are not ruined in the event that a reader disagrees with their methods.

My goal is to level with you in a valuable way that doesn't turn you off from finishing this short book. Investigating residential cases is a passion of mine that can change people's lives for the better or worse if not done properly. Because I know these cases come with the potentially severe consequences, perhaps it means that I take this hobby (as others call it) too seriously, but that's something I have to deal with. I would rather deal with a case with sterile gloves than carelessly be a bull in a china shop in someone's home.

Several parapsychologists, researchers, and investigators in this field have inspired me. You won't see them starring in any reality series (yet), but you will be able to find their published works online and their methods on their websites. In the back of this book, you will find a list of recommended reading and I strongly suggest that you go and buy these books right now. Don't wait until you finish this book.

If you're a seasoned paranormal investigator who is researching different approaches to cases, this book is for you. If you're brand new to paranormal investigating and not sure how to get started in working on residential cases, this book is definitely for you. It is my hope that all of the readers of this book gain a positive experience, learn something new, and get a dose of reality as they dive into working cases involving the paranormal community. In fact, when it comes to working residential cases, it isn't the deceased or the phenomenon that you should be afraid of, but you should fear the living.

CHAPTER 1
WHAT'S THE DIFFERENCE?

You've been on numerous investigations in public locations, you've been on more ghost tours than you can shake a stick at, and you finally want to make that transition to investigating the paranormal and helping people with their haunting. Surely there isn't much of a difference between investigating the haunted house that does nightly tours and a person's house with a similar haunting.

Well, there's a big difference.

Let's role-play. Because I'm an actor and I enjoy these kind of exercises, let's have a Haunting A and a Haunting B. A is in a public location that does nightly ghost tours and hunts for a price and B is in a private residence that includes a husband, wife, two children, and a dog. The exact same phenomenon is happening but the context is completely different.

How do you dress when you arrive to the location?

What kind of questions do you ask the owners of the space?

What kind of questions and provocation techniques do you use on the entities?

Do you implement any resolution methods?

Because the context of A and B are different, therefore you must approach these two hauntings in a different manner. I admit that I enjoy investigations of public places because it takes a level of pressure off of my team and me. We're free to establish communication with the other side in our own way without worrying about the repercussions to the client.

And that right there will be the biggest difference between a public and private investigation.

When you're working on a residential case, the way you approach and communicate with the presence will directly affect the clients. I feel many investigators miss that when they take on cases. After they decide to provoke a negative entity, the investigators pack up and go home at the end of the night. But the clients are the one who will be stuck at home with the phenomenon. This is why approaching these cases cautiously is very important, especially in a case that involves children. It can be dangerous to jump right in on a case and ask direct and invasive questions of the phenomenon. Especially if the phenomenon is negative or evil, trying to barge in with proton packs and getting rid of the phenomenon in a single night may only make things worse.

The main problem in the field right now is that people want to imitate what they see on paranormal reality television because it's easy. It could be because the investigator is being naïve or just lazy. But when it comes to working residential cases, there is no room for laziness. In fact, you'll most likely be physically and mentally exhausted at times from working residential cases. This is a completely different realm of paranormal investigating that isn't discussed often.

Many investigators and researchers will stick to just investigating public locations because they do not want to deal with the responsibility of dealing with clients and their personal lives. And that is completely okay. You can be a paranormal investigator and researcher without trying to help clients. You can create breakthrough methods and technology from investigating for the public. It takes a special kind of dedication to want to help people with their personal phenomenon and I applaud investigators who want to take that unique challenge.

But there is a completely different context and landscape once you move from the world of public locations to the residential cases and it can be quite overwhelming at first. However, if you know the difference in environments and circumstances then you are already well on your way to being an effective investigator who is ready to help people with their hauntings. This can be invaluable to those who are dealing with the unknown and they have no one who understands what they're going through. You are that answer to their pleas and prayers.

The Business of People

Whether you're working the public or private sector, being in the paranormal community means that you will be working with a lot of different people with numerous types of personalities. Personally, I find that working in public locations means that I can focus on what my team is doing without being observed by a client. This gives my team room to make mistakes and work out any kinks before walking into a private home.

When you take on a residential case, you are being looked at as the expert in the unknown. The client will look to you for answers. If your team is disorganized and doesn't look like they know what they're doing, the client won't be confident in you or the resolutions you want to implement.

When I bring new team members into residential investigations, they only observe and I'm honest with the client and let them know that there is a trainee on the team. All of my clients have been satisfied with that. And, so far, has been successful. It offers a unique experience to the members training for the team and I've given a level of transparency to my client thereby earning their trust.

If your entire team is new and inexperienced, it's best that they get their first few investigations out of the way in the public arena. That's the time to mess up, talk about it, and learn from the experience. Most importantly, when mistakes are made, it's best to address the issue and move on. For the sake of yourself and your team, be sure to surround yourself with members who are open to criticism and are comfortable with giving you feedback. If you're a director or founder for a team, you must be open to constructive criticism as well as the occasional unprofessional person who has to let you know that everything you're doing is wrong.

Volume Isn't Everything

Television has been very deceptive and has made many investigators and ghost hunters believe that a case can be solved in a single visit or weekend. While there are certainly cases out there that can be resolved in a short span, there are many cases where it's an ongoing investigation for a few weeks or longer.

That was my first wakeup call when I started doing casework with a team in Orange County in 2008. This particular team received cases on a regular basis, and soon enough, the cases started to overlap each other. The director was getting frustrated because these cases were not closing easily and the time commitment to the team began to get more intense. I was in my junior year of college in San Diego, still working and doing theatre, and the commute north was becoming too much for me. Because this team wanted to maintain a reputation for taking cases in the double digits per month, the team members had no choice but to continue. I eventually had to resign.

Instead of working on one or two cases at a time, this team wanted to work on several cases at a time so that they could use the numbers in their advertising in order to get more cases. When teams are advertising their services (while essentially competing against other teams) the focus tends to be on the number of cases instead of the time spent on research and thoroughly working on a case. I disagree with this tactic.

Slow and steady wins the race with these cases while speedy work often results in sloppy work. If you're dealing with a case where the clients are just curious about a benevolent presence, you can probably close that one in a timely manner. But if you're dealing with something dark and malevolent, bringing in a priest to do a blessing isn't a one-stop shop for everyone. If you don't know what you're dealing with because you rushed through the case, how do you know that the solution you're implementing is even going to work?

Now, the timeframe for dealing with cases will also depend on the manpower you have and the clients. If you have a large team that is dedicated with free time, you can probably get through evidence and research in a good timeframe. But if you're like most people, you and your team members have day jobs, families, and other obligations that need to be fulfilled. Paranormal investigating can easily become a full-time hobby and keeping your life centered is key to being an objective investigator.

I've met teams who dedicate their entire existence to the paranormal while overlooking their families and their day jobs. If the investigator isn't well rounded and doesn't go out into the "real" world (so to speak) and, fails to focus on other areas of their life, it can be a counter-productive activity. Volume isn't as important as time. An investigator who has worked on 100 cases in the last 10 years has much more experience and street smarts than the investigator who has done 100 cases in 6 months. Of course the more time that passes by, the more experience and knowledge the investigator has gained, and in a way, can then deal with cases more quickly and efficiently.

For my team, we usually give a turnaround time of about one to two weeks to go through evidence and about three to four weeks to close a case. This may seem like a very long time and it is. After the first visit, if phenomenon is confirmed, the client has to deal with the validation of his/her suspicions that there is a potential haunting now shown by a team of experienced investigators. Most often the timeframe will be determined by the urgency of the case and the client's availability.

When it comes to going through evidence, I've found that taking breaks often helps prevent the mind and eyes from going stagnant and seeing and hearing things that aren't there. We also have team members who weren't present at the investigation who help with evidence review as a fresh set of eyes. When we're not actively investigating, we're researching the land, property, the people, or going through evidence as soon as it's in our hands.

Knowing Who You're Talking To

I also tend to not jump into cases immediately because I would like to have some sort of idea of whom I might be talking to, as the purpose of a client investigation is to validate and bring a resolution. I've learned that asking the same standard questions such as...

"Who are you?"
"Why are you here?"
"Are you a man or a woman?"

"How old are you?"
"Can you say my name?"
"Can you make a noise for me?"
"Can you give us a sign of your presence?"

…can lead to stagnant investigating. When you don't get an answer, what do you do? If you run into this, it may be time to change your questions or what you're saying to the unknown presence.

If possible, I like to get the history of the house and the land so that I can work with a specific time period. This is inspired from John Sabol's "ghost excavations" where he works with scenarios while excavating and exploring haunted locations. He approaches areas in the mindset of, "This happened here, and what remains?" Mr. Sabol doesn't investigate or work with residential cases but his methodologies can be used for private investigations.

For me, this makes sense. If you walk into a client investigation with a specific scenario to work with and present yourself in the context of the deceased, it opens the line of communication more efficiently. It makes you more than just a paranormal investigator in someone's house. It removes you as an outsider.

Sometimes the information and the resources may not be available. So, then, yes…you are working blind. Ultimately you have to use what method works for you and what helps you productively work with the client.

When it comes to investigating a public location, there will often already be resources to look into with regards to the history of the property and information on who is haunting the location. But even though the location seems to have already done the work for you, your job isn't done yet. Unfortunately there has been recent issues of deception occurring in the field and if you don't check into legends and stories properly, you may risk your reputation.

Keep an Eye Out

Public locations may often embellish the history of the property or the people who maybe haunting the location for the purposes of garnering more business. If that is the case, then the deceased person you're trying to communicate with may not even exist. In that case, any evidence or data you collect will be completely flawed. If you then post your findings online, anyone who may know better will call you out.

To avoid this issue, do your research before even beginning to investigate a public location. You can use the venue's information as a starting point, but be sure to dig deep into the research yourself. Not only will you find a deeper appreciation for the location, but you will also be able to correlate any people who were linked to the location with any deceased person reported to still be there.

If you do run into discrepancies, you and your team must decide together how to move forward. In an age where paranormal locations, teams, and guides can be exposed on the Internet in an instant, business can be ruined. There have been several investigators and experts whose reputations have been destroyed both intentionally and unintentionally. If you have no interest in engaging in drama then the best thing to do is either walk away from the location quietly or investigate it anyway and correlate the experienced phenomenon with the accurate findings you did obtain. Approaching questionable locations in this manner sometimes results in new discoveries that the location can use for their ghost hunts in the future, which benefits both groups.

When the Cases Aren't Coming In

I like to do public investigations whenever there's a break, meaning that there aren't any private cases to work on. It also gives your team a good break from working on private cases where there may be a lot of pressure and your team must perform well for the purposes of having a successful closure of a case. This is also a good time for team bonding and having your team members get used to each other and building up trust in each other.

I also like to give my team monthly research topics so that they're still involved in the community. Many of my team members actually do a lot of solo work in the paranormal and we all come together when a client needs us. By doing independent work and research separate from the team, it keeps your team members knowledgeable along with being well practiced in investigation techniques when you're not working on cases. It also helps your team members to learn from each other and try out new techniques or methodologies that you've come up with, or have run across in your research.

I've found that my most valuable learning experiences have taken place at public locations. I learned how to work with strangers and I learned what to do and what not to do on investigations. When working in a group at a public location, you will find that many people will try to imitate what they see on television. There is nothing wrong with that as paranormal reality has become sort of a gateway into this kind of world and if you scoff or make them feel humiliated for their actions, they will be turned off to the world of the paranormal completely and that is counter-productive. Paranormal reality shows are being imitated by those who are just starting. While I do not recommend starting out in the field in this way, it isn't right to be mean to those who are seen doing that in public.

I learned best from those that lead by example. In my early days when I noticed that there were investigators doing public ghost hunts, I watched them. And the ones who stood out to me the most were the ones who had completely unconventional approaches to investigating. One investigator in particular stood out to me because she was the only one not carrying any fancy technology around to communicate with the dead. Instead she just had a voice recorder where she recorded notes for herself and she wrote notes down in a notebook. This investigator inspired me to approach an investigation in a "stripped" fashion. But I'll divulge more in the evidence chapter when it comes to equipment and evidence collection for a private residential case.

Having confidence in what you are doing will stand out much more in a sea of people who are trying to learn from imitation.

In closing, while there are many similarities between investigating public locations vs. residential cases, these two areas are not the same, and should not be approached as such. Essentially, between you and your team (if you have one), prepare your own approach and methodology to working with clients along with public investigating. Customize your investigations accordingly to each client and the reported phenomenon that is occurring. In fact, I can say confidently that each residential case that I've worked on with my team has been a different experience each time. Even with cases that have a similar occurrence going on, the resolution is never the same.

As you continue further in this book, I'll discuss other aspects of working with residential cases through my own personal "war stories" that I've experienced by myself or with my team. It is my hope that you learn from these war stories and avoid the issues from them. You would not approach a demonic case the same way that you would approach a poltergeist case, nor would you use the same resolution for a little girl haunting a home as you would for a spirit that is lost and has no idea on how to move on or cross over. The same thing goes for even a public venue. Approach things differently each time with a clean slate and try not to imitate what you saw on television.

CHAPTER 2
THE HUMAN MIND

The biggest aspect to consider when taking on residential cases is the fact that you will have a tremendous amount of influence and power on your hands. You will be brought in, as the experts, and your expertise will bear a significant amount of weight in what you tell your clients. This is why it is exceptionally important to avoid diagnosing a case before you have had a chance to actually be there in person. So often, I run into clients who talked to a ghost hunter on the phone, and were told to consult a demonologist based on the client testimony.

By doing this, the ghost hunter in question (we'll call him Bob) already tainted the client's perspective on their paranormal phenomenon. Because Bob told the client to consult a demonologist before even visiting the household, now my team has to first rule out a demon. It is a necessary extra step because the client not has the perception that there is something evil in their home. Client testimony is one of the most valuable tools when coming up with a solution for a case. When my team has their initial interview with our clients, we have to consider testimony in two ways.

1. It is [usually] the client's perspective and experience with their phenomenon, how it is making them feel, and how it affects their everyday life.
2. Client testimony has the potential to be extremely biased. This is true especially if the client watches paranormal entertainment such as horror films or reality television. The client may be looking for key elements to see if they're haunted and may not even realize it.

So if a ghost hunter like Bob tells a client right off the bat to seek a demonologist, he is making a very drastic diagnosis without proper examination. Doctors don't tell their patients to get tested for emphysema if they call the office concerned about a cough. If you don't feel comfortable taking on a case whether it is because you think the client is crazy or the case may be too much for you, then have resources readily available to give to the client.

Your resources can include other teams you can send the client to, as well as psychic mediums who specialize in case work, religious clergy who are open to the paranormal, local authorities, counselors, and medical professionals.

Under-Promise and Over-Deliver

When I was working in retail during college, I was in the sales department for appliances. It wasn't the most glamorous job on the market, but it paid the bills and worked around school. One of the most memorable things my supervisor told me was "under-promise and over-deliver." The reason why he pretty much pounded this concept into our minds was to avoid returns and refunds, which lost the company money.

To apply this philosophy to working residential cases, if you over-promise to a client, guaranteeing them that you will be able to get rid of the ghost, demon, etc. for them, you are setting yourself up for a situation where you cannot make mistakes or fail. Over-promising usually means under-delivering which can be devastating to the client that is coming to you for help. To put it bluntly, don't ever make promises to the client, except for the promise that you will do everything in your power to help them. Don't promise to eliminate the ghost, don't promise that the client won't need any more sleep medication, and don't promise that the client will be free from any future paranormal activity.

This may seem harsh, but the reasoning behind it is that paranormal phenomenon is not a one-way street. Accountability on the client's part will be essential as well. But more on that later.

If you, or you have team member who constantly made promises to our clients without the team's knowledge, this behavior needs to stop. Of course on the outside, this can seem very professional and makes the team look like they have it all together. But eventually it will make a mess out of your cases.

Hypothetically, say you have a team member who enthusiastically takes on the role of case manager (CM). But you begin to notice that the CM gets incredibly hostile if another team member wants to speak with the clients for their own notes and clarification. For the case in the hypothetical scenario, you discover that there is drug use involved, which the CM didn't disclose to you. After speaking with the client yourself, you discover the CM guarantees that the phenomenon will stop and they won't need rehab or their psychiatric medication. The drug use alone should force you to let go of the case because it would jeopardize the safety of the team. If you have a team member that over promises to the client and is secretive with their interactions with the client, it might be best to let them go.

Based on the hypothetical situation, both the client and the team are disappointed and let down. But what it all comes down to is that the CM ignored the personal dynamics and behaviors of the client that was contributing to the phenomenon, making it extremely complex. The CM also withheld information from the team and the director that could have affected their safety, all while promising the client that the team would be able to take care of the case. Unfortunately, if the CM promised that the team could get rid of the phenomenon, the client could find validation in continuing their drug use as well as justify discontinuing medication for psychological ailments. This is an incredibly dangerous situation, and also helps us in seeing the extreme consequences of making promises that you might not be able to keep.

Should this hypothetical situation ever become a reality, skip the drama and have the team not take the case, recommend other teams, and give the client helpful resources that would help improve the their personal life.

The Affecting of Private Lives

When you take on a residential case, it is more than just spending some time on the phone and a night or two at the client's house. The client has invited you to spend some time in their personal lives including their habits, their history (both the good and the bad), and their living situation. I often learn more about the personal lives of my clients than I know some of my friends. But in order to properly work on a case, this type of intimacy must be formed.

You may also learn family secrets that you dare not utter to the client's spouse or children. If it's a possible contributing factor to the phenomenon, sometimes you will learn information like that on a "need to know" basis. Our team signs confidentiality agreements, and the client signs paperwork too that acknowledges the fact that if we learn certain information that could potentially lead to danger or harming of others, we have no choice but to report it. It's important to make that clear, have the conversation, and get that paperwork out of the way before moving forward.

Essentially, when you and your team decide to take on residential cases, you will be immersed into the private lives of complete strangers. Your presence may even raise tensions within a family, especially in a situation where a spouse doesn't believe in the activity that is taking place. You may even find yourself and your team members playing with the client's children or pets. The important thing to remember when in the midst of this immersion is to keep your professionalism at an all-time high. It can be easy to become informal and casual, and while there are moments for that, remember that you have a job to do. If you blur the client-investigator relationship, it could lead to other problems in the future.

Coping With Validation

When you work with a client, you're there to confirm or debunk their experiences as paranormal phenomenon. The majority of our clients are more relieved if we're able to debunk the phenomenon that is occurring. Hence why it is crucial to do a walk-thru of the house on your first visit. If the client states that they're hearing footsteps following them around on the top floor, check the floorboards and see if it's not the wood resetting. If the client reports feeling dizzy in the office, check the electromagnetic field (EMF) levels, especially if there are a lot of electronics in the room. High EMF levels could result in having paranormal-like experiences and hallucinations, but it's the brain reacting to the EMF.

On a separate note: while many individuals and teams may disagree, my team still uses an EMF meter. But we don't use it for ghost detection. We use it for the actual purpose of detecting electromagnetic fields around the house and looking for fluctuations in the electronics.

When the team has similar experiences as the client and we're not able to explain it, we have given a form of validation to the client, which can be a lot to handle. For the client, it can be a relief to know that they are not crazy, but it is also disturbing to them because there really is something going on that they can't see or explain. We find that sometimes we have to give the client some time to process what is happening before moving forward, if circumstances allow it. If it's not a malevolent haunting, we usually give the clients a day or two to contemplate and react before moving forward while checking in daily. Having your haunting confirmed by a team of experts can be a lot to handle by itself. Don't rush the client into the next step. Respect the time they will need to take it all in. The client will also have a lot of questions for you at this time, so make yourself available when possible to be there.

Empower and Educate

Coming in and taking care of the phenomenon is one thing, but directing your clients to other educational resources is exceptionally valuable. You know the saying, "Give a man a fish; feed him for a day. Teach him how to fish and you feed him for a lifetime." A big part of resolving cases is empowering the clients to take control of their lives and their homes. You want the client to feel confident and empowered enough to communicate their boundaries, as well as be educated.

Educating the client means that you let the client know what was afflicting them, explain and debunk any phenomenon that wasn't paranormal, counsel the client on how their actions and personal lives may have contributed to the activity (without a negative spin or placing blame) and finally, educating them on what they can do in the future to either avoid or resolve their own phenomenon. I've started keeping a book list on hand to give to the client as well as a list of websites and documentaries that could give the client some more knowledge. As the saying goes, "Knowledge is power."

Of course this doesn't mean that you give the client all of these tools and resources so that you never have to talk to them again or follow up. [If education and empowerment aren't already included as team goals, consider adding it.] I've been fortunate enough to collaborate and communicate with several investigators who do similar things, such as Brian D. Parsons with his highly effective E4 method for working residential cases.

Investigating a Residential Case

Finally, I want to briefly discuss methodologies of investigating a residential case. With the rise of paranormal television, there is a trend of removing the clients from the house, turning off all of the lights, and seemingly solving the case in a weekend. I'm not necessarily saying that this method is incorrect, but it makes me think, "Oh, in a perfect world..."

My team tests and tries out different methodologies and theories, taking the bits and pieces that work best for us. I have a great amount of respect for people like Brian D. Parsons who has been able to devise his own methodology and practice for residential cases, and will credit him wherever possible since my team, the Association of Paranormal Study, has had the most productive investigations since adapting aspects the E4 method into our client work.

The first thing I want to stress is that it doesn't have to be dark outside for a productive investigation to occur. Depending on team member or client availability, sometimes the only time you have in the residence is during the daytime. All hope is not lost with this. When you interview your client, you may find that much of the activity happens during the day anyway. And you want to be able to experience and document the activity in its "natural" state.

Speaking of "natural" state, we keep our clients around whenever possible. I have found that as the investigator being in the house only a few times, if the phenomenon is intelligent, it will already identify my team and me as the outsiders. I first learned this concept from John Sabol, who devised the Ghost Excavation approach to investigating. If the presence sees us as the outsiders, it is likely that they will not respond to us if we ask broad questions or provoke (which is against our team standards). Having the client with you and participating to the extent of their comfort level will help initiate communication and bring about a response. Oftentimes, the client wants to observe our process, which we welcome.

If the client has been experiencing a phenomenon for several months, or even years, it is likely that the case won't be resolved in just a day. Sometimes, it may even take a series of trial and error when it comes to prayers, blessings, and cleansings. Much of the solution will depend on your client and how confident they feel in the solution process. This goes back to the chapter title of "The Human Mind", you must exude confidence in the solutions that you are exercising without overpromising. I've found that investigating the client's home or business is just a small part of the solutions process, which is why many teams don't pursue client work for very long after starting. There's much less pressure when investigating a public location than there is taking on a residential case.

Your resolution methods may not be effective at the first try. That is okay and it means that you need to try again. The last thing you want is for the client to feel blame or guilt because they didn't believe in the cleansing and blessing that took place, thus taking a jab at their confidence and psyche. It's a fine line to walk, but being honest with the client and letting them know that they have an important role in the solutions process will help alleviate their fear and make them feel empowered.

The Power of Influence

This chapter is meant to emphasize how much influence and power you have when you decide to work on residential cases. If you become alarmed or scared, and the client is there, you must retain your professionalism and objectively document everything that happens so that you can help the people who called you there in the first place. I suppose you could call it a superhero complex, but you have to be strong for others. Nothing will make a client feel more hopeless than seeing the experts they called in running away in fear. Many times the client will already be psychologically exhausted and you are the key to their peace of mind.

When you are out there doing client work, remember that your words, advice, and actions have power and meaning behind them. Even if you're having a bad day, or you really are scared of what could be at the residence in question, you have to find a way to manage it. As our team says sometimes, "Suck it up, Buttercup." Now this doesn't mean that you have to check your humanity at the door, but this is also the cost of taking on residential cases. I always tell my newer members that if they are feeling scared or vulnerable, they are free to step outside to collect themselves and have a quiet moment to recharge. It's okay to be scared, but it is how you handle your fear that's most important in residential work.

As you embark on your career as an investigator who works with residential cases, keep a journal to keep track of your feelings, findings, and experiences. This will prove to be invaluable in the future as you continue to work on these types of cases and can be a valuable resource for your team should you decide to share it. I also encourage you to have your team journal out their feelings and experiences during each case.

I have found that residential casework can be very rewarding. Not only do you feel good about helping your community, but you always learn something new with every case. While there's a cliché saying in the paranormal that, "there are no experts", there are people who have much more experience and education than others. I personally don't believe that there are no experts. I believe that if you dedicate yourself to an area and continue to research, study, and examine it on a regular basis, you can become an expert. The most respected experts acknowledge that they don't know everything and continue to learn new things with each new case study.

CHAPTER 3
EQUIPMENT & EVIDENCE

Surely when it comes to the use of technology in paranormal investigation, there have been both great strides and great setbacks. With the help of reality television, people who want to attempt to document tangible evidence of anomalous phenomenon have a guide on what to purchase and use to capture said occurrences.

Unfortunately, it seems that there have been misconceptions when it comes to using technical equipment. For one, much of the equipment that is used in the entertainment side of paranormal investigation is mostly ineffective. But why in the world would these television shows use this equipment if it didn't actually work? Well, let's remember that the entertainment industry is for just that...entertainment. In this chapter, I'm going to loosely go over what essentially makes up the basic "ghost hunter" kit (or pack), what you should avoid, and people whose work you should follow for the latest innovations in tech that is actually effective.

Know the Purpose

The most important thing you need to understand when it comes to your equipment is the true intention for why it was invented in the first place. The majority of the equipment that is used today wasn't made for capturing ghostly evidence, but rather for more conventional purposes. There is a difference between how something works and why it was invented. This may require some time with the owner's manual as well as some research at your local library and online, but once you know how your equipment works, you'll have a leg up on many other investigation and ghost hunting teams out there. What amazes me is the fact that there are teams and individuals out there who will blindly use this equipment knowing only what they saw on television and will take whatever they capture as hard evidence of the paranormal, when it can be explained and debunked in a matter of seconds at first glance or after a cursory.

The majority of investigators miss the big picture by focusing on the debunkable evidence and wasting time arguing against logic and reason to prove that the light reflection they captured was really their dead grandmother. Making it worse are the psychics who will try to confirm it as well, thus furthering the insanity and encouraging these setbacks to continue.

Expensive vs. Cheap Equipment

Another common question I receive involves whether or not teams should invest in hefty amounts of money for their work or cause. The great investigators from the early days didn't have thousands of dollars in equipment when they were going out and helping families. All you need to get started is a pen, pencil, and paper. Taking copious notes of the client's experiences, your experiences, reported activity, and just on the case overall is incredibly useful.

However, in the recent years of investigating, it has turned into an evidence-centric field. And if you do experience something that is unexplainable, having some sort of documentation may even help further the field and legitimize paranormal research. So, we return to the question of how much money to spend on equipment...

There is no simple answer, except this: you get what you pay for. A $10 audio recorder won't capture as much audio evidence as something more expensive. [With better and more sensitive mics, better access to different frequencies...you clearly have the potential to capture clearer, stronger evidence.] Again, if evidence collection will be a major component of your team and you want to share it publicly, you might want to invest in better equipment that will show clarity. There is nothing more frustrating than looking at a team's evidence online and finding out that their evidence was captured with very low quality equipment with results that are so fuzzy, you wouldn't be surprised if there were a lot of false positives, meaning that the person thought they caught an anomaly only to find out it can be logically explained. False positives can only bring about teachable moments, but will do you and your team no favors if you're trying to present yourself as a serious team cut out for residential cases.

Photography

I'll start off with the area that I'm the most knowledgeable in because I am a photographer (check out "Alex Matsuo Photography"). This also merges with the concept of orbs since digital photography seems to have brought on more orbs than film cameras could ever imagine. I use my camera for both my photography business and my paranormal investigations. This means I use interchangeable lenses and lighting equipment to a certain extent. Anytime you introduce a flash into a dark investigation, you will most likely get a lot of orbs and shadows. If you're going to use any kind of camera, whether it is a DSLR or a "point and shoot" camera, you need to have a basic understanding of how your camera works as well as the mechanics of lightings. Once you understand how lighting and reflections work, you will be a step ahead of many teams.

It is my firm belief that every investigator needs to take a basic photography course online. There are several free resources online, or better yet, connect with a professional photographer. When I capture anomalies, I don't show it to paranormal investigators or enthusiasts, I show it to my photography colleagues and ask them "what happened" in the photo. They will be able to dissect a photo to a degree that is almost superhuman. Professional photographers can tell you which angle each light anomaly came from and what might have caused it. There will be at least one photographer or two that will be happy to assist. You just have to look and ask, specifically the ones that teach courses or are very interactive on their social media sites. Make sure you butter them up with compliments on their work.

Also, be very aware of matrixing and pareidolia. Have you ever looked up into the clouds and seen a dog or some other design, animal, human, creature, etc.? Then you have experienced matrixing/pareidolia. It's crucial to become familiar with this concept, as many "paranormal" photos you may receive from followers and clients may be no more than their brains creating familiar patterns out of a pixilated mess.

Speaking of client-submitted photos, you also want to become very familiar with ghost apps. Obviously not for personal use, but for the sole purpose of being able to detect a clever photo that is obviously fake. I've seen the ghost app photos fool even my most seasoned researcher colleagues. There is nothing bad about being fooled, since the ghost apps are still fairly new, but knowledge is power. Fool me once, shame on you. Fool me twice, shame on me. If the person who submitted the photo insists that it is legitimate, and several individuals have created charts of the ghost app ghosts, then I recommend sending the chart to them to prove your point.

About 99% of the orbs that you capture on your camera are explainable. This goes back to having basic knowledge of photography and knowing the difference between a true anomaly and dust, moisture, light, lens flare, etc. The last thing you want to do is show a client a photo of an orb and try to pass that off as evidence of their haunting. Now, I won't say that ALL orbs are explainable, because I've witnessed unexplainable orbs that I've seen with my naked eye. When I take a photo, it looks like a random light in the midst of darkness. If the lights are on, it's even more interesting because it emits its own light with no plausible source.

The whole orb phenomenon came from television. Paranormal

investigations normally take hours on end, and for television they have to be condensed into 30 minute to 1-hour episodes, so you see all of the "interesting" stuff. But any seasoned investigator will tell you that there are some investigations that are a bust and nothing happens. So what do television shows do? They have to keep up the ratings, so they will create their own paranormal phenomenon. Dust is everywhere and it can make an appearance not only in your still photos, but also in your video work.

Video

Continuing the orb debate from the photography section, you need to understand how dust works. There's a running joke on taking "perfect orb photos" and it involves rustling all the furniture and shuffling through carpet and then turning on the night vision mode on your cameras and let it fly. If there are numerous "orbs" in a single shot on your video camera, it is most likely dust and dander. If there's smoke or mist in the video, check to make sure no one is smoking and there are no possible sources for the anomaly like warm air in cold air, etc.

Sony, for whatever reason, has stopped including night vision in their conventional handheld camcorders. I managed to snag a few on Amazon and EBay used, and when I have the money, I try to buy more since they are becoming a rarity. Otherwise, all you'll really have to rely on for night vision are security cameras, which stay stationary for the most part.

Again, like with photography, you need to become familiar with how light works in video. These devices interpret light differently than our naked eye. And night vision is even more different. Become familiar with how anomalies work by purposely trying to create your own orbs, shadow people, etc. Obviously don't put this stuff online to the public and try to pass it off as legitimate evidence. But if you can become familiar with explainable anomalies, you can avoid the hazard of false negatives.

If you really have cash to burn, investing in a thermal camera is a good idea. The most common brand is FLIR and they create very good cameras. The most common experience clients share is temperature change, whether they are getting colder or warmer. APS has temperature guns to check in, but they can only do so much. Having a thermal camera on hand to monitor the situation will help you gauge whether there is a significant temperature drop taking place.

The best and really the only advice I can give you in video technology is you may need to invest some cash in this area of technology. Understand the basics in video and the dangers of recording over the same file again and again and how it can create double layering. That walking shadow you thought you caught at that last investigation? That was your team member walking down the sidewalk after a previous investigation. Of course, the chances of this in digital are significantly less than recording with film, but it has been known to happen on occasion.

Audio

The bread and butter of paranormal investigations have been electronic voice phenomenon, also known as EVP. Voices from beyond are not only chilling, but they can be very tangible pieces of evidence. If you can get a recording of an anomalous being saying your name, giving facts that no one else would know about, answering questions, etc. then that can be a great stride in paranormal research.

While many investigators use simple handheld recorders, there have been hardcore researchers who have invented devices that can better capture spirit voices. One such individual is John Mizzi. If you don't know who he is, connect with him on Facebook. I have interviewed him on several of my podcasts and he does get results. This brings me into another point. If you find that your current tech isn't giving you the results that you want, create your own accessories that will help in your research.

The normal decorum in conducting an EVP session during an investigation is asking a question and waiting for about 15 seconds in between. With any extra (and explainable) noises that come up, such as a car driving by, a rumbling stomach, etc. you MUST tag those sounds so you can avoid those false negatives in your evidence review.

A device that I recommend that all teams look into is a real time EVP recorder. What this device does is play back the recordings in real time on your investigation, so that if you get a response to one of your questions, or even a response from some action that you're doing, you can proceed and keep going on that topic. Not only does this make your investigations and interactions more productive, but you avoid missing opportunities as you do your evidence review. There is nothing more heartbreaking than getting a response to a question, not knowing what the answer was, and then continuing with another question and leaving the person on the other side hanging.

Luckily in this department, you can go cheap or go expensive. You will get as much out of audio tech as you put into it, and I don't just mean monetarily, but also in terms of spending time with your audio evidence and researching the area.

What APS does in audio evidence review, is share our files with each other with no information. If time is of the essence, we will share timestamps of interest or just the direct clips. It is important to not influence each other by saying what we think is being said. If we're together in the same room, we will write down what we hear in the clip, otherwise, the team will email their thoughts directly to me and then I will post the results on our file-sharing page. If there ends up being correlations, even better.

Become familiar in the different classes of EVPs. The clearest and best EVPs' are called "Class A", meaning that no editing or enhancements are needed and you can hear exactly what is being said. "Class B" will usually mean that some volume enhancements are needed and there "might" be some differences in interpretation, but there will be common denominators. "Class C" will require a bit more help in the editing process and there may be disagreements in what is being said. There are classes in D and beyond, but at that point, it might be best to just toss the evidence. If there are major disagreements in what is being said and a substantial amount of editing is needed so that a voice or anomaly can even be heard, there might not be anything there. At that point, you're chalking it up to matrixing audio.

The Big Reveal

Obviously tech has the potential to be overwhelming, especially with evidence. Tech review takes several hours, and even more so if you don't know what you're looking at or hearing. Become familiar in basic sound concepts, that way you can looking for anomalous sound waves and be able to find EVPs more efficiently. Take breaks while looking at photos and video so that your mind doesn't start playing tricks on you and you start seeing things that aren't there. Breaking the work up amongst your team members helps too. Have your team over for evidence review, bring snacks, and take happy breaks.

The final part of your investigation will likely involve a "reveal" to the client, meaning that you're sharing your findings of the investigation with your client, thus providing some validation of their experiences. Some teams will show their evidence before providing solutions and others will provide the evidence after a solution has gone into effect. If the client wants the activity to stop, APS will reveal the evidence first and then proceed forward with the resolution. The reason behind this is that sometimes revisiting the activity and the phenomenon after implementing a resolution can be an invitation for the presence to return, as it's retaining a piece of the past experience and making it present.

Most of our clients don't want to keep their evidence, as they want to move forward beyond the experience and never deal with it again. Other clients will want to keep their evidence. When this happens, make sure you ask them why, and mention the potential repercussions of holding onto the evidence. Our team clearly states in our paperwork that the evidence both belongs to APS and the client, and if the client wants to make their evidence public or shop around to television shows, they have to credit us as the team that captured it. Sometimes clients will want the evidence to show to their friends and family. Just make sure you mention the potential setbacks that may ensue from keeping the evidence and that way there are no surprises.

Going Public

The last thing this chapter will cover is posting your evidence publicly. APS made the decision to not post our evidence publicly, no matter how remarkable it may be. I find that the more interesting my evidence may be, the closer I keep it to my chest. Know that with any decision to go public, you are making yourself vulnerable to criticism. The focus of APS is not to capture the best evidence, but come up with the best solutions for our client. If the client just wants to capture evidence of the ghost in their home, while we may still go, we won't post the evidence online. This is mostly due to our client confidentiality agreement as well, because you never know who knows who and who may recognize that living room in the video you posted.

Always get permission from your client in writing before posting evidence. As a paranormal investigator and researcher, I highly discourage posting locations and client names. The client may not want their friends and family to know what was going on, they may not want their coworkers to know...it's a sensitive subject. If you do have a team that posts evidence online, make sure you also block out any family photos or any obvious decor that could violate confidentiality like names, certificates, etc. Hackers have become quite smart on zooming in on blurry things like college degrees and get the full names of people. Plus knowing what's inside the home can give away personal information like potential salary and location. It's the little things that can give away so much.

CHAPTER 4
PROTECTING YOURSELF

This is a rather vague title for a topic that encompasses many areas when running a paranormal investigation team. Before embarking on your first investigation with a team that you founded yourself or a team that you just joined, there are different loose ends of protocol that need to be tied up. While these recommendations may seem like a hassle or a bother to take care of, they will not only protect you spiritually, but legally as well. Last time I checked, no one really wants to go to court or engage in spiritual warfare. Both of these scenarios are not helpful and will keep you distracted from conducting a more productive team.

There are a series of things you will have to get together logistically before you embark on even your first investigation. If you are reading this book, I am assuming that you want to take on the residential cases where you will be entering people's homes and businesses, engaging with members of the family, and temporarily inserting yourself into the lives of your clients.

This chapter will first get the paranormal stuff out of the way and discuss ways and offer suggestions to spiritually protect yourself. Then the remainder of the chapter will be on how to legally protect your team and your clients.

Shielding: Yes or No?

To start off, you need to decide where you stand spiritually. First of all, you have to decide for yourself what role religion plays in the paranormal, and whether "will and intent" plays a role in phenomenon or not. "Will and intent" has connections in shamanism where the human psyche and mind has the power to change and make things happen around you. Think of the idea of "like attracts like" and if you put a desire out into the Universe (or

God), it could come true. If you're not settled in what you believe in, you won't be able to effectively help your clients. Reason being is that you are the expert being called into the case, and the client is looking to you for the solution. What if the solution is a religious one? If you're not confident in the resolution that is implemented, how can you expect the client to jump on board?

Whether you are a follower of Christianity, Islam, Judaism, etc., you need to be grounded in your faith, whatever it may be. To be honest, being a part of the paranormal community has forced me to question my own religious beliefs in terms of, "Is Christianity the only way?" because I saw practices from other religions be just as effective as Christian methods.

I was raised Southern Baptist, but after starting college and being more exposed to other religious beliefs, I've learned it is just a part of not only growing up and becoming independent, but also the paranormal world. It's quite jarring the first time you watch a resolution get implemented that doesn't involve the deity that you were raised to believe in and worship. I will admit that I sort of went through an identity crisis because of it. It took a few years to finally be comfortable with the fact that my religious belief wasn't the only way.

To state the obvious, religion is important for many. People have changed their lives for it and even killed in the name of their belief. When you are dealing with the paranormal, it is a spiritual battle so to speak. Now, this doesn't necessarily mean good versus evil, but you are going into an investigation as a means of "conflict management" between the client and the presence that is affecting them. Sometimes, you will find that your case is basically miscommunication. The client may have done something to attract the presence, or they reminded the ghost of a lost loved one, or they need to convey a message. These are the favorable cases for the team because they have a positive conclusion, and the client is more empowered by perceiving the case in a different way besides the typical, "My house is haunted and the ghost is scary." But, of course, the paranormal field is never simple, and sometimes you have to deal with a case that is more complex, negative, or both. So, you need to protect yourself spiritually.

I often believe that when you're an investigator and researcher, you have a shiny sign above your head that only spirits can see that says, "Come talk to me!" Sometimes I get transients, meaning that I'll have a spirit or some sort of presence in my home temporarily before they move on to another location. If I have a psychic around, then it intensifies because there's someone there who can listen. Of course, this could all probably be cleared up with an investigation, but I don't do that to my home, which is also known as my sanctuary.

I've had ghost transients as well as some pretty nasty entities sent my way by people who wanted to interrupt my work. I've learned that there is a great value in shielding and grounding yourself not only in intense casework, but also in your normal everyday life. I'm not here to give you exercises or a "how to" on this, as I feel that it is a personal choice and path. You will find that giving your grounding and shielding your personal touch will make it more effective. The exercises that I use come from different sources and suggestions that I've read and discussed with others in the field.

Grounding for me is centering yourself and bringing balance to your life. People ground themselves through meditation and prayer. As someone who deals with anxiety, grounding helps relax me and reminds me of who I am, what I want to achieve for the moment, and affirming that I have the power to bring in positivity to my life and to those around me. Shielding is establishing your spiritual boundaries and building a wall. I like to shield myself in a way where only positive things can penetrate my personal bubble. I like to visualize a bubble of white light around me. Sometimes, if I find myself getting upset or feeling threatened, I close my eyes and strengthen my bubble.

Grounding and shielding also does more for your personal life than just your paranormal career. Working in education, which can sometimes be a chaotic environment, grounding and shielding has become a necessity. When psychic Katie Weaver did a reading on me, she asked me if I worked with kids. After I told her yes, she said she saw many strings around me, representing attachments to my students. It just goes to show that there is energy wherever you go, even in the work place. When you're entering into a case, don't underestimate whatever you might be dealing with. Even if there is nothing paranormal or abnormal going on, the energy of the client will affect you no matter what, whether it's positive or negative.

There has been debate among investigators about whether we should shield ourselves on cases. I personally believe that if I have my shields up too aggressively, I won't have any sort of experience or be open to the activity that the client is experiencing. But at the same time, I don't want to carry that case back home with me in any other form besides my notes and paperwork.

I tend to not shield myself before going into a case, and if I feel necessary, I'll do my usual ritual of leaving it all outside my home before stepping in. Much of it is visualization-centric for me where I close my eyes and I picture air coming out of my pores, releasing all the negative energy from my body and soul. I'll also say a prayer to God to seal the deal.

Granted, if I know I'm going to walk into a negative case, I prepare myself not only logistically but also spiritually. However, this is just my own personal deal. If you don't believe in the demonic or the concept of negative entities, that is completely fine and acceptable. But you have to understand that your client most likely does, and you'll need to formulate a compassionate game plan to either convert the client to your ideals or find a compromise and meet in the middle.

Legal Protection

You must decide what kind of "business" you want your team to be. I cannot stress this enough. Teams have gone in the non-profit direction as well as the LLC way. First, you have to decide what kind of work your team is going to be performing. In any situation where you're going to be put in people's homes, you're making yourself vulnerable to a lawsuit. You have to be exceptionally careful with how you speak to your clients and what kind of services you are offering.

Do not advertise your services as expert or licensed. There is a reason for this in terms of liability. Unless you have a licensed mental health professional who is willing to use their credentials and help you with clients, you are not qualified to offer any advice in terms of mental health or medication. Even if you have personal experience with psychological issues and different kinds of medication, you have no leg to stand on if you go to court. In fact, offering any kind of advice by telling a client to change their medication or diagnosing them with a mental illness could get you sued.

When the team gets a case, we do ask that the client disclose their mental history along with what medications they are taking. It is not uncommon for us to turn down a case and advise a client to see a mental health professional. Not only do we not want to put ourselves in a vulnerable position legally, but we also believe that the paranormal phenomenon that the individual may think they're experiencing may actually be a side effect to their medication. If we tell the client that the ghosts are real, they may disregard anything that their doctor tells them, and may even stop taking their medication. This can have a disastrous affect.

This also means that you have to be honest with your client as well in terms of your medical background. If you still decide to pursue the case, you will need to be in touch with a family member or a trusted friend of the client who is willing to let you know when things may get unstable. You will also need to have the client sign paperwork.

In terms of paperwork, you will need to get a contract that releases you of any liability. This includes damage to the property, stolen items, and whether or not the client can sue you for various reasons including mental health, integrity of the family unit, and satisfaction with the case progression and conclusion. We ask our clients to take inventory of all of their valuables, and we give them a choice on whether or not they want to stay in the house during the investigation. I usually prefer the clients stay because then they are witnesses to the events. While my team has yet to be accused of stealing jewelry or anything of value, I often hear of teams going through this situation. When you put some responsibility on the client, by asking them to either remove the valuables or keep them put, these sort of situations can be avoided.

Background Checks for Your Team

When assembling your team, you need to make sure you know every nook and cranny of each person's history. This includes mental health, criminal history, and academic record. This may seem like common sense, but there are numerous teams out there that don't conduct these background checks. APS originally didn't do background checks, and it wasn't until 2013, two years after the team started, that I started doing them. We had discussed background checks, but didn't start until we had an incident. It was due to a former team member who had caused some strife within our dynamic. Another team member had a hunch and decided to search for their name in the local court system and found that the team member had a history of being sued for various reason. Granted, this was a fairly minor issue, but this showed that there can be internal issues that you won't pick up on from personal interaction alone.

It doesn't matter how smart or educated anyone may seem, they could have a criminal record that includes theft, pedophilia, or assault. None of these traits are acceptable in a team member. Unfortunately, if there is a potential team member that has an accusation against them, I will likely not take them on. It isn't worth the risk that I would be imposing on my team's reputation, as well as the safety of my members and clients. When you take on a case, the client is putting their trust into you, and they shouldn't need to worry about whether they have a thief or a child molester in their home.

Unless you have the budget to pay a company for a background check, most employers will provide a copy of the background check for your team member. You can also do a lot of digging through background check websites, the county court system, and social media. I do encourage you to either get a free trial on a background check website, or pay the fees to get this done. This will relieve worry and prevent headaches in the future. If a team member gets to the interview phase, I require that they show their identification card, social security card, school identification, etc. Basically anything to prove their identity. I'll also ask them if there has been a recent background check conducted on them, and if I can have a copy. When doing this, be aware of fraud. The copy from the applicant can be a starting point to help you go deeper.

It is vital that you ask for this information up front before interviewing. I interviewed a prospective team member who ended up stalking me as well as sexually harassing me. When I reported the incidents to the police, I didn't have a valid address, phone number, or real name to go by. After doing an Internet search through various terms such as name, screen name, email address, etc., I found that the prospective team member had a history of harassing females, and clearly showed signs of mental illness. When this man threatened to rape me if I didn't quit the paranormal, I was able to get the police's attention to pursue him harder, and a restraining order was issued with no contest from the prospective team member.

This is all to protect yourself and your team. It is ensuring that there is nothing on the record that can make your team vulnerable to an attack that could damage the reputation of the group. In the paranormal, your good name is everything.

Background Checks for Clients

This next section is a bit tricky. Just as you want to do a background check on all of your team members, you want to do research on your potential clients. On our case submission form, we ask for phone number, name, email, and address. Even though we are unable to do official background checks, we can gather enough information to at least look the client up on the Internet via social media and seek out any information about recent arrests, etc. We do this because we want to know what kind of situation we are walking into. We don't know if the client will try to rob us, or intentionally put us in a situation where they can sue us. This background check is solely for the protection of your team.

As previously stated, the other important thing we ask on our client submission is a list of medications along with any health diagnosis. This is to also factor in any psychological and physical health problems that could affect our case. For example, if the client is diagnosed as bipolar or having schizophrenia, you have another dynamic to deal with, as we have already discussed. Typically, we will decline cases where mental illness is involved. They tend to be too complicated by having too many variables when determining exactly what is going on with the client.

However, if you feel that there is something paranormal going on with the case, and you wish to pursue it, you will need to come up with paperwork to clear you of any potential liability. Using an attorney would be helpful in this case, because the last thing you need is to be dragged to court for aggravating a mental patient. Along with the paperwork, you will need to talk to a friend or family member involved with the client who is of sound mind. These will be the testimonies that you will take into consideration for your case. Then, on the night of the investigation, the client with the psychological issues should not be present. If you feel that you can eventually integrate this client into the investigation, then use your best judgment and go ahead. I don't typically recommend this, but if you feel strongly enough to pursue the case, this is a way to protect yourself.

I must repeat this. If you take on the case, *do not* offer any advice in regards to medications or treatment, even if you or a team member is a licensed professional. I heavily recommend involving the doctor treating the client to make sure that you would not be doing anything to make their situation worse. The doctor may discourage you from taking on the case and I would listen to their advice.

On another note, if the client has any history of using illegal drugs, you will need to make sure that not only is the client clean, but also that the property is completely clear of any drug paraphernalia, and to sign a document saying so. Unfortunately, this is a situation where my team has direct experience that I briefly mentioned in Chapter 2. The trajectory of this case was full of deceit and the client was not being completely honest with us until we showed up to the site and realized exactly what they were getting themselves into. I was on the other side of the country at this point and advising from a distance. I ignored my better judgment and we learned a very valuable lesson. The client had a history of using various drugs including meth and cocaine. I discovered that this client was very paranoid, constantly watching their surveillance cameras, and anything that was pixelated had to be a demon. The client's stories kept changing from angels to possession, and it became extraordinarily difficult to keep a cohesive timeline of any activity. Anytime we attempted to advise or implement any sort of resolution, it didn't work because the client didn't follow through. When the team arrived on site, paraphernalia was discovered, putting APS in a vulnerable position. Eventually, we had to walk away, and the client threatened to sue us for not solving the case. I had to declare that they were free to take us to court, but that we would be sharing our testimony to the authorities in regards to the drug use. We never heard from them again.

Because of this experience, I discourage taking on a case where there is any recent drug use in less than a year. I understand that people have histories and difficult times in their lives where they need to do something to ease the pain and struggle, and that habit can be hard to overcome. But again, this falls in the realm of trying to protect your team. Not to mention that drugs can also cause brain damage that could have similar effects to experiencing paranormal phenomenon. If a case like this is pursued, I recommend informing the client that not only do they need to be clean, but that if there are any drugs or paraphernalia found, the team will vacate the premises immediately and call the police. If the client is genuine, they should not have a problem with this. If there is an issue, do not take the case. It is not worth the safety of your team, or the possibility of being arrested in an unexpected drug sweep that's on the same night as your investigation.

One final note on a case such as this: If you have team members who are aware of the risks and are okay with going on this kind of case, have them sign additional paperwork that states the situation and risks point-by-point. You don't need to be sued by your team members because you put them in an unsafe situation that they were not aware of. Honesty is the best policy, and you should have a group that not only has the team's best interest at heart, but yours as well.

As you can see, there are numerous variables in the world of client work in the paranormal field where you can be vulnerable to being attacked. By arming yourself with knowledge, paperwork, and confidence, you will have the ability to make the best decision for the well-being of your team both physically and spiritually. Your team will have confidence in you as the director or member because they know that you will support and defend them, and that their safety is your number one priority. This will also help boost your team morale. If you're going to investigate the darkness and the complexity of the paranormal world, knowing that the person going into battle beside you has your back will make the case work much more bearable, and you will all work together as one cohesive unit.

CHAPTER 5
DEALING WITH DRAMA

Within the paranormal community, there seems to be a wealth of drama everywhere, especially on social media. I will admit that I have been guilty of getting too caught up in arguments over social media about the legitimacy of evidence, or even the integrity of several members of the paranormal. I learned the hard way that it is best to just smile and stay out of it. Even if you have good intentions, the person seeking your help may not have a positive response and then you are faced with someone slandering you. Because of how sketchy members of the paranormal community can be, I advise my team members to stay out of online arguments. I've never had to follow up on this, as my team has learned from my experience.

On a similar note, if someone writes to you directly about another individual, do not respond. I have found that trolls such as these are seeking attention and looking for some sort of validation for their actions. You reap what you sow. If you engage in constant negative activity, you will continue to stew in that, and you'll end up having to claw your way out. But if you remain neutral and foster a positive and encouraging environment, it will benefit you in the end and you will have a lot of peace within your team and the community. Another saying I particularly enjoy is, "Don't dish it if you can't take it." I have found that a lot of people who are out there dedicated to "exposing" people for their wrongdoings live in glass houses themselves. Don't get me wrong, if there is someone purposely scamming others out there, then they need to be exposed and need to take responsibility for their actions. But before even going about this, you have to decide whether the repercussions and backlash you'll experience is worth it. Most of the time it isn't, unless you were scammed out of money personally. Even if you feel that someone is taking advantage of people's good will by scamming them out of money, unless you have solid proof, anything you say in a public venue could be interpreted as stirring the pot, or worse, spreading rumors that might not be true. Solid proof tends to be lacking when it comes to these allegations, which will put you at risk should there be no justification for any of the accusations. I recommend staying out of it in general because not only does it tarnish your reputation, but it takes time away from your own research and team.

I was extraordinarily hesitant to write this chapter, as it would be forcing me to relive and rehash situations in my team that nearly destroyed the organization from the inside. It also exposes a time where APS wasn't quite as mature in how we handled issues and drama. Sometimes we have to learn the hard way. Since one of the themes of this book is learning from mistakes, I hope this helps you avoid the situations I list here. As Abraham Lincoln said, "A house divided against itself cannot stand," and if your team is having internal issues, then any external problems that may arise could cause permanent damage to your reputation and psyche.

Drama within Your Team

There will be a time when you will experience drama within your team. Depending on how big your group is, it is inevitable that there may be disagreements to the point where it eventually explodes. I have had a few team members that ended up teaching me a lot about how to run things and I will discuss some of the times where there was drama within our team and what we did to resolve it so that we could be functioning once again. Should you ever find yourself unable to perform your duties, make sure that whoever takes over for you has the best interest of the team, and don't let it be someone brand new to the group regardless of length of investigation experience.

To avoid drama within your team, keep an eye on whether they bad-mouth of individuals or other teams. There is room for disagreements in a civil matter, but there is a clear difference between creating drama and expressing concerns. If you have a new team member that wants to dive in head first, transition them gradually and gauge their reaction regardless of whether they signed the paperwork already. I had never been a fan of forcing people to prove themselves or their loyalty, but after that experience, I can see why it's done. Because, someone will sneak past the guarded lines, and potentially cause major disaster.

Don't reveal passwords or access to sensitive information to anything linked with personal email accounts, bank statements, etc. to new members. It is best to keep that information to yourself (as the director), and eventually, when you bring on a team member trustworthy enough to take on the extra responsibility and will respect the confidentiality agreement.

Should you find yourself in a position where there is drama between you and another group or outside person, ensure that the rest of the team stays out of it. Don't expel too much energy on damage control and privately contacting a large amount of people as a last ditch effort to preserve your reputation. Sometimes, you ultimately have to let your good name stand on itself. Those who know you and your team will continue to support you. Those who walk away are better off walking away, and there is no need to chase after them and force them to stay.

How to Handle Members Who Don't Get Along

This is one of those unfortunate situations where I have to step up and tell the fighting team members that while they are not required to like each other, they must respect each other and the team dynamic. This means not gossiping or bad-mouthing the person to other team members as a way to gain supporters. If I find out this is happening, then I give the team member one last chance to change their behavior, apologize to the person and the team members they spoke to, or stepping down. Again, this is a team where you need 110% of trust in each other, and if there are any doubts, it can disrupt the dynamic of the team.

I have been blessed to have a team where this has not happened. There was one instance where a team member quit due to constant disagreements with another member, but he acknowledged that it was an issue he needed to resolve on his own. It was a clean break with no hard feelings. I wish all disagreements ended this way. As the director, I have to be very firm when it comes to team dynamics and any pending drama. Of course, this may come across as micro-managing a bit, but when the morale of your members are at risk, you have to protect it.

Protecting team morale is eliminating the poison from the dynamic. This means keeping an eye on your team members to see who seems to be engaged in arguments and drama on a regular basis. This also includes hearing judgmental statements from them on a regular basis. Look at it this way, if this person is comfortable gossiping and speaking badly about others to you, it's only a matter of time before you do something to anger them and they do the same thing to you. It's the golden rule of treating others the way you want to be treated. If you are in a leadership position within your team, it is your job to remain neutral and make decisions based on what's best for the team and not your friendships. It can be extraordinarily hard, but if you surround yourself with people that you trust, it will help.

A book that I find as an excellent resource when it comes to your judgments and snap decisions is the book *Blink* by Malcom Gladwell. In the book, Gladwell talks about the science behind snap judgments and first impressions. Ultimately, you have to trust your gut. If you feel that someone is lying to you or may not be the best fit for your team, then trust that feeling. I've found that the times that I ignored that "sinking feeling" within me was when that person eventually brought about a lot of heartache and hurt.

When Your Team Members Are Married

Oftentimes, you will get co-applicants who are in a relationship or married. This is perfectly fine in my opinion. I would advise letting the couple know of the risks of investigating as a couple, and how sometimes the darker cases can take a toll on relationships. Checking in with these team members often during the difficult cases is encouraged. Not only does this show that you care, but you can also gauge how your members are doing psychologically and emotionally. If there's a situation where the relationship ends up breaking apart, all I ask of these team members is to keep personal business outside of the team. This may result in one of the team members quitting the team, but in cases such as these, it's a personal matter. It is best not to force the member to stay when they feel emotionally they cannot handle it. I also recommend leave of absences before making a final decision.

If a couple is in the midst of fighting or breaking up, stay out of it. If one or both of pair tries to involve the team, it may be time for a conversation of whether they should continue to be a part of the team or not. Do not give relationship advice as a member of the team, and don't try to fix a broken relationship. There are professionals who deal with matters such as this, and the last thing you want is to be blamed for a failed marriage or relationship.

Under no circumstance do I allow personal dynamics to be displayed while investigating a case in front of a client or a public venue in front of community members or fellow investigators from other teams. Professionally speaking, if the couple can't handle keeping it together for several hours, then they do not go on the case. Luckily, I haven't had to deal with this too much, but I have heard of teams where this is a regular occurrence and I hope this little section can be helpful. Sometimes these situations are out of your control, and do not reflect the quality of your group.

Trash Talking vs. Expressing Concerns

But what about those times where a team member has a legitimate concern? I've learned that there is a distinct difference between talking trash about someone and expressing a genuine concern about the team. While you don't want to encourage bad-mouthing and possibly compromising the trust within your team, you also want to foster an environment where your team can approach you should there be an issue going on that you're not aware of.

The first trait of a genuine concern is that the member hasn't spoken to anyone else about the issue. This means that they have kept their concerns private and aren't trying to gather "an army" of supporters to assist with their cause.

The second trait is the yearning for privacy regarding the matter. They are not interested in humiliating the team member and are actively seeking a resolution. They might even request a private meeting with you overseeing while they discuss their concerns with the other member, while keeping privacy and confidentiality a value to uphold. After the meeting has concluded the issue is not brought up again. This member is willing to move on and not hold grudges, depending on the severity of the situation.

The third trait is that the team member is willing to hear the other side of the story. They acknowledge that they could be mistaken in interpreting actions, or that there was a misunderstanding. I try to uphold the principle of making my team function with professionalism, love, and grace. This means that we know that sometimes members may have bad days, but instead of responding with aggression, harsh judgments, and assumptions, we acknowledge that perhaps we might also hold some responsibility for the situation. No one is perfect.

This is all pending on what kind of issue needs to be resolved. There are some "no tolerance" situations that may lead to immediate dismissal of a team member such as assault, breaking confidentiality, or bringing in a poisonous and toxic environment to the team dynamic. When a team member approaches you with concerns, do not immediately dismiss it as gossip or trying to stir the drama pot, because that could damage the trust that is shared between you two. The fact that they are willing to speak with you in a private setting is enough to want to take some time to hear out the concern. If the concern comes out in a group setting, then pull the member aside so that there is a private discussion rather than keeping it all out in the open.

We have all had bad experiences with people in some way or another. While the past drama in my team left me wounded, injuries do heal with time, and we have become a stronger team because of that situation.

This may seem basic, or feel like you're herding kittens, but sometimes it is a necessary monster to address when running a paranormal team. There will be dynamics outside of the team that will try to make its way in, and there will be issues within the group on occasion. Making your stance known early on when a new member joins the team will help alleviate the drama that may come by. And when problems do arise, you'll be able to handle them on a case-by-case basis. But know that if there is drama within your team, you will have done everything in your power to prevent it. Hopefully, this chapter will be a waste of paper and you won't ever have to come back to it.

CHAPTER 6
APPROACHING & INVESTIGATING A CASE

When APS embarks on a case, we typically recruit clients from online. However, since we do have a phone number listed, I will usually field calls from people who aren't quite as computer savvy. This is completely okay but eventually we do try to direct the client to our online submission form where they can tell us, in their words, what has been going on. In the situation where it is not possible for the client to fill out the online form, then we put the phone on speaker and take copious notes, filled with follow up questions. We also get permission from the client to record the phone call. This is done so that the case manager (typically the person fielding the submissions and gathering the information to present to the director) can do a check to make sure they have gotten as much information as possible.

Regardless of how much information the client divulges in their case submission, a follow up call will occur from the case manager or the director. This is to ensure authenticity and consistency of the client's testimony.

Depending on the severity of the case, the beginning process can include the following:

1. **Initial Contact**: This is where first contact is made. This can be done either through a phone call, or responding to a case request online.

2. **Response & Gathering Information:** This is where the case manager or director will respond to the initial contact. It is at this point where we refer the client to fill out the online case submission, or conduct a phone call to gather the information and learn of the severity of the case. This should come from

any witnesses who are willing to speak with you, or at least a gathering of names for follow up, if the client permits and doesn't violate their confidentiality. I prefer to have the client fill out a case submission first before hearing their voice. It is a personal preference so I can better gauge the case. Of course I'm human and sometimes will pass judgment on the case too early if I hear the client's voice in telling their experience. It is also an interesting process to assess the client's writing and then hear them recount their experiences verbally. Conducting interviews via Skype can help gauge a potential case.

3. **Presentation of Information to the Director:** The case manager will discuss the situation with the director, where arrangements for the investigation are made.

4. **Contacting Professionals:** If the case includes a concern with mental health, APS will usually avoid the case, as we do not give any medical diagnosis or recommendations. There are teams that will require this on all cases regardless, and if you have the resources, by all means use them! The clients who are legitimate will oblige to the request of getting a mental health evaluation, but also be cautious that the request could create a risk of being sued. However, there are some situations where this won't be able to happen, so proceed with caution. If the client feels that they need some sort of religious resolution such as a prayer, cleansing, deliverance, exorcism, etc., it is best to contact someone sooner rather than later so that there isn't much waiting between the investigation and resolution.

5. **Presenting Information to the Team:** This is going to depend on how much knowledge of the case you want your team to have. Typically, the case manager will know all the dynamics along with myself. I will give a general overview to my non-psychic team members, but leave details out to see if that information arises during the investigation. This will all depend on the case dynamic, and I change this approach depending on whether there is a negative presence or not.

After the testimonies are collected, the investigation aspect can begin. Be sure to leave plenty of time to arrive at the residence or business on time. I do not allow my team members to wear any logos or anything that would let on that we are a paranormal group. Keeping your client's confidentiality in mind is key to establishing a professional relationship that is built on trust. Leave the logos for paranormal conventions and meetings.

When it comes to the actual investigation, I could write paragraphs with a step-by-step on the process. Instead, I will tell you key things you will need to work through in order to give the client what they need, not necessarily what they want.

First of all, as stated earlier in the book, you need to be clear on what your team does. If all you want to do is collect evidence, make that crystal clear. There have been so many clients who have felt like they were hung out to dry because a team came in, collected evidence, then left without providing any sort of resolution. This is where the feelings of betrayal, loss, and resentment towards the field start.

Ultimately, you are being called in to help assist in determining whether there is paranormal phenomenon. Not only that, but once it is determined that there is something anomalous occurring, then you must try to figure out why it is occurring. It is very similar to an intervention or mediation between two conflicting parties. Otherwise, the client will be left with not only with a lack of solution, but not even knowing what they are doing to cause the activity. This risks in a reoccurrence of the activity by the same entity, and leaves the client back at square one.

If you conduct EVP sessions where you are asking questions, the goal is to try to identify who you are talking to, what gender they are, age, and if possible, finding a name. The same goes for spirit box sessions, photography, videography, and divination. Of course, you need to know what you're looking at, and what you're interpreting in terms of results. I want to emphasize that none of these tools are hardcore scientific tools. They are basic tools to help gather information. Using technical equipment does not make you a scientific team. But, just because your team is not scientific does not mean that you are not doing good work.

Using Psychics

Another tool that is popularly used within teams is the use of psychic mediums. Again, this is another tool that can be used, and should not be the only tool that is used. If your team has a resident psychic, or a psychic that you use on a regular basis, of course make sure that they are not in some sort of compromising position where their lack of knowledge of a case is compromised. It is best to leave all psychics cold to information before coming into the investigation. If possible, even ask the clients to leave for about 30 minutes, or have another team member take them to a different part of the property or neighborhood to gather more information. You want to keep your psychic work objective.

We will turn picture frames around so that the psychic doesn't even know who is in the household. We will let the psychic know that the case involves children once they see the evidence of a child's presence (for example, their bedrooms).

If you're working with a new psychic, you will need to interview them, and get to know how they work early on before you bring them on to a case. You don't want to have the psychic do something to compromise the integrity of the investigation. For example, I brought in a psychic, I'll call her Abby, for an APS case in California that was especially negative and dark to the point that the family was all sleeping together in the living room. I spent some time talking with her via email and over the phone informing her of the family's fear. While I didn't tell her the nature of the case, I told her how the investigation worked, and felt comfortable enough to bring her onto the case.

When Abby arrived, she ended up bringing multiple people with her to the investigation. Instead of the two we agreed upon, I had five psychics wandering the property. The clients had gone out to lunch during this time. When it was just APS and the mini team of psychics, there was no dialogue, and Abby didn't want to divulge the information she was picking up on *yet*. This was a red flag, and given that the situation was now including ten people in one house, tensions were high. When I asked Abby when she would be ready to share the information, she said when the clients came home.

A Recipe for Disaster

In this situation, I had lost control as the director and head of the team. I couldn't gather the information I needed to judge the case and Abby's abilities. Looking back, I should have put my foot down and requested the information, but in the interest of trying to avoid conflict, I allowed the behavior to continue. When the clients arrived home, Abby took the family and started wandering the house, telling them that there were fairies in the rooms, and that the client's husband had his deceased grandmother hanging out in the master bedroom. Abby also told the family that the son was a beacon of light for the dead and that they should just "get used to it." While Abby didn't have to believe that there was a negative presence, she lacked the empathy to try to calm the family's fears and told them that their fear was irrational.

At this point, Abby completely made the investigation about her and her attempt to show off her abilities, with her group watching. Instead of offering clarity or something to calm the client, the family was now more scared than ever. I asked Abby for some sort of blocking, shielding, or coping methods for the family if she really believed that the 2-year old son was a "beacon". She handed them a piece of paper with shielding techniques, left copious amounts of business cards all over the house, and bid us all goodbye. I was stunned. APS felt very taken advantage of and the clients felt as if everything took a step backwards.

This experience caused me to go through psychics with a fine-toothed comb. It also taught me to always maintain control of the investigation, no matter what. I can never allow control to leave my team like that ever again, for the sake of not only the APS name, but for our clients. There is no shame in questioning and evaluating a guest before allowing them to come into the investigation. I will be a control freak if it means that my clients are in good hands with those who have their best interest at heart.

I hope that this experience will help other directors, and even team members, maintain control of their investigation. Don't let anyone else try to upstage your work or any progress you have made. Since that experience, I make it very clear to the psychic, or outside investigators, that they are guests on MY team's investigation, and they must respect the protocol of the team. I haven't had this issue since.

On the same note, if you are ever called into a case as a psychic, consultant, and guest investigator, ask the director or liaison how the team functions. You don't want to create animosity by stepping on toes or unintentionally crossing lines. It's all about respect and by keeping communication open.

The conclusion of the case was that there was something anomalous occurring. I ended up bringing in another psychic who specialized in house cleansings, protections, and blessings. She was exceptionally sympathetic and understanding of the family's feelings, and was able to counsel and offer advice for after the case was over.

Calling In Other Experts

When APS first approaches a case where the client is reporting footsteps, popping, cracks, electrical abnormalities, we will check the house. If no one on your team has experience in the contracting world, there are workshops, classes, and online tutorials that can show you signs of an unstable foundation, loose boards, etc. When it comes to the electrical anomalies, I recommend calling in an electrician because no one in your group needs to get electrocuted.

From my education and training in theatre, I already know how to check for faulty wiring, but I will not fix it. I will inform the client to call in an electrician since that could be a liability issue. If you're not comfortable checking into the house or property, calling in a contractor is the next best thing. Many contractors will do free consultations, or even come by pro bono if they're interested in the work that your team does. It's about creating a good working relationships with members of the community. Just as you want to create a good networking partnership with counselors, psychologists, and psychiatrists, you want to do the same for contractors and electricians.

Types of Investigations

There are two different types of investigating that you will do while you are working on the case. These two types are passive and active investigating. These aren't specific methodologies, but more of labeling what you're probably already doing.

1. **Active Investigating:** This is the type of investigating where you are engaged and responding. This could include asking questions, conducting spirit box and EVP sessions, using a psychic, basically anything to promote an active conversation with whatever presence is in the house. Not only is this about asking questions and responding, but truly listening to learn, not listening for the sake of talking again. This can be a wonderful opportunity to get to know what you're dealing with, and determine whether it is a positive or negative influence.

2. **Passive Investigating:** This is the kind of investigation where you are not actively involved, but you have recording devices on with trigger objects such as toys or music present. You are not there to actively engage with the phenomenon, but recording what is going on when you and the clients are not looking. This is where evidence review will be key. If the client has reported strange noises occurring where no one is present, objects moving, etc. then passive investigating will be key in collecting information.

I've often been asked whether to have the client removed from the home during the investigation. I say no because usually the phenomenon that is occurring is usually connected to the client. Having the client recreate their actions from when they had experiences also has the ability to trigger the event all over again. The times I have had a client leave the space (note: not the property) was usually when I wanted to take a closer look at an occurrence, or if the client was disruptive and preventing us from doing our job. The only time I'll have the client leave is when I have a psychic in the house and I let them do a supervised walkthrough. This helps me gauge the psychic's accuracy, and whether it is appropriate to allow them to speak to the client.

Boundaries & Lines

When you are working a residential case, you are the expert that is called in. As I mentioned in the beginning of the book, your words have power. But your actions will speak louder than your words. If you feel like you're in way over your head at any time, there is no shame in calling in another team or an expert. You can either pass the case on, or stick around to be there for support for the team and your client. I have found that clients will be quick to connect with us. It could be because we tend to be friendly and open-minded. Think about the situation from your client's perspective. They were experiencing this unknown phenomenon, and finally there are people with them who believe in the unknown.

Be very careful of this, while it is initially positive. You want to set boundaries as well. While you want to be available to answer questions and help your client in any way possible, when they start to call in the middle of the night, sending numerous emails in a short period of time, or requesting more of your time than you're able to give then reevaluation will be necessary. While you're doing a community service, you don't want to sacrifice your own life to the point where your personal and professional relationships will suffer because all of your focus is on a high maintenance client.

Also, while you are investigating a case, the client is a client. If you connect as friends, you need to hold off until the investigation is over, and even until after the case is closed. You want to maintain a professional relationship not only get your job done, but to also avoid liabilities.

In cases where we are investigating the home or business of a friend or family member of a teammate, we have to do our best to maintain the professionalism. The teammate will often have to take a step back and not be so active in the investigation since they biased emotionally and with regards to evidence. This will have an impact on how your investigation goes. Only in dramatic circumstances would I ask the team member to take a step back completely. Usually, I'm more than happy to accommodate, as long as the functionality of the team isn't compromised.

Case Reports

As soon as we conclude the first visit to the client's property, we start our case reports with a meeting to discuss our approach. Case reports include important information such as:

- Client name
- Address of property
- Phone number & email
- Description of the client's experiences
- Questions for the client
- Hypothesis
- Questions to ask the presence
- Contextual ideas to use during investigation
- Equipment used
- Investigators present
- Investigator's experiences

- Was the approach successful? If not, why?
- Anomalies captured & timestamp of occurrence(s)
- Investigator's thoughts & theories
- Dynamic in the client's unit (family/workplace) before the investigation
- Dynamic of unit after the investigation
- Resolution implemented
- Concluding thoughts

You might detect a few traces of the scientific method. Does this mean that APS is a scientific team? No. It means that we are exploring different possibilities by approaching the case with an objective to try to solve the mystery of the case and resolve it. Also, in the event that the authorities are ever called into the client's home or there is a pending case regarding a separate incident, if we're asked to provide information to the authorities, we will hand over our case reports.

We will do our best to start our investigations off with a strong foot, open communication with the client, and build a rapport of professionalism. With the paranormal becoming a bit "tongue in cheek" thanks to the variety of television shows, we want to show that this is a field that needs to be taken seriously.

CHAPTER 7
HISTORICAL RESEARCH

This is perhaps one of the most important chapters of the book, but it might even be the subject that brings about the most apprehension. You have to do some sort of historical research whether you are investigating a public building or a private residence. Why? This will help you figure out what is going on inside the house and put you on the path of better solving your case. You have to know what has happened in the state, city, county, and property before the client moved in. You never know what might have happened in the past to contribute to the current activity. From finding out who founded the town, to finding out what sorts of activities took place on the land, there is a plethora of information that will benefit your case.

There are many places where you can start researching. Your most accessible option is using search engines on the Internet. Keep in mind that this shouldn't be your only option, even though search engines can be excellent with their results. I personally have memberships to newspaper archive sites as well as genealogy sites where I can do more digging from home and get leads before I head to the local library of the client. Local research will be most effective by visiting not only libraries, but historical societies and county court houses as well if you need more information in regards to previous owners and land records. I recommend designating one or two people to do this sort of work, especially since it can be daunting at times. If you have a few team members who are passionate about research and are enthusiastic about it, let them do it. I say this because historical research can be overwhelming to someone who isn't passionate about it, and if they don't enjoy the work, it won't be done well and you might lose a team member shortly after.

There are numerous resources out there to give advice and insight on historical research, but there are bare basics that you need to be aware of before starting to dive into this crucial area of investigating. Luckily, the Internet has an array of people out there who are more than happy to give support and tips should you find yourself hitting brick walls and you need information in a pinch. While this may not be shocking, there are a lot of paranormal investigators who actually work at historical societies and libraries, and therefore are surrounded by information on a daily basis.

Learning the Land

As the investigator, you owe it to your client to know as much historical information as possible. APS likes to start big and work our way in. We will start with the state's history and its significance in American history as well as lore and urban legends in certain areas. We will then move into the county and town and look into the following:

- What year was the town/city founded?
- Who founded it?
- Was the town known by any different name?
- What kind of tragedies have occurred there?
- What does the town's history population growth or decline involve?
- Was the town known to have a lot of fighting, brawls, affairs, death?
- What are the urban legends of the local area? Town ghost stories?
- Has the town experience any catastrophic events like fires, flooding, earthquakes, tornados, hurricanes?
- Has there been any widespread death from a famine, illness, murder?
- Was the town ever located somewhere else?

Many of these questions can be answered by searching on the internet. If you want to dive deeper, you can make notations of significant people and historical events and then go to the library to check out the microfilm to see what the newspapers have to say about it. If you can't initially find information in the local town paper, expand your horizons to the nearest city to see if they covered the event or incident. As soon as you can answer the above questions to the best of your abilities, you can start to hone in on the client's property. A special note: I don't ever identify myself as a paranormal investigator or ghost hunter when contacting third parties. Let's be honest, not everyone is open to the possibility of the paranormal, and ghost hunters have been getting a rather dubious reputation in the last few years. Don't close the door on yourself by taking this kind of risk.

When honing in on the history of the client's home or business, you will need to research land deeds. This is usually the part of the historical research process that gives us the most headaches. If the county has their records online, by all means start there and get the index entry information so you can go to the courthouse and look in the actual deed books. Your path of success will be to go backwards, meaning that you start with the most recent order and go backwards in time. You'll get the most information including names, price, and land descriptions this way. You can track how the land has changed, if it expanded or shrunk in anyway, and how these transactions worked out. Sometimes local hauntings are blamed on miscommunication and sketchy business deals regarding land.

You will also need to get used to reading land deeds. They won't say, "5 acres of land with 5 trees", but instead they will have descriptions in terms of N, S, E, and W with degrees, including rocks, trees, brooks, creeks, lakes, etc. It will take practice to read this, and there are great books out there to help you learn. Once you get the dates on these purchases, note what year that structures begin to appear, and once you have that, cross reference the year to see what county the land was in at the time. You will feel like you're going in circles at times, but you will know every inch of your client's property inside and out.

At APS, we tend to cover a lot of military cases, which means that records are usually sealed. We will still research as much as we are able before we start hitting brick walls thanks to the government. The information is usually enough to know what happened on the land, and events that happened before the base and clients moved in.

This may seem like a pain, but this is exceptionally valuable. You want to go into the property with names and events, as this will help you engage with the phenomenon and ask the appropriate questions when you're investigating. I find that doing the research after the investigation means a lot of missed opportunities for more productive conversation.

Genealogy

The first thing I recommend is becoming friends with a genealogist. They have made it a career to help people find more information about their families and relatives. It is a complex and yet beautiful craft of research. Luckily for the paranormal community, there are many genealogists involved who are more than happy to offer their services pro bono (I do recommend giving them an honorarium for their time as a gesture of thanks).

If you don't have a genealogist available, then you will need to do the leg work on your own. Looking back on the wonderful land deed research you did earlier, you can now take the names and start punching them into the computer. I tend to take the public history of haunted locations with a grain of salt. This doesn't mean that they are lying, but some will make declarations in regards to how and where the previous owner died and that will be it. If you're investigating a location where a family member served in the military, you might have the luxury of more detailed state-owned records as well as the National Archive if you're researching an era where record-keeping is more reliable.

You want to look into each family member, where they lived, how long they lived in the building/land, if they had children, and where they died. You will find yourself creating a family tree, or several if the property has been own by numerous people. And of course once you get the names, then you can cross reference them with your historical research on the town to see if they were ever covered by the newspaper or had influence on the town. If you're at a location with a cemetery on the property or nearby, you might be able to visit the graves of the people you might be trying to communicate with. With genealogy, you can gain more insight than just names on a piece of paper. Instead, you can dive into the personal stories that may explain why the location is haunted.

From your time in the genealogy world, you will probably find out more about a family than your very own. If you are dealing with a case that involves a recent death, then the people you are researching will be there right before your eyes. You will essentially become a member of their family from the research you do, and perhaps even expose a few family secrets by accident. Use caution and your best judgment in cases such as these. If the information is pertinent to the conclusion of the case, then speak with an authority on your team. Depending on the information that could be exposed, selecting a family member based on their stance and relationship within the family unit will be your route.

Contacting Landlords & Former Owners

This section is particularly tricky. Essentially, you want to know if the people who previously lived or worked in the location had had experiences, but you don't want to violate your client's privacy. In this situation, I see it as a last resort. If you're finding that the activity started within the first day or two of the client moving in, and they had never experienced any paranormal activity previously, there might be reason to believe that the paranormal activity was already present prior to moving in. Before going door-to-door or calling the client's landlord and asking if any of the previous tenants experienced anything weird, you will want to get permission from your clients to talk to outside people.

Even after you get the permission, you will need to approach these people with caution. Immediately asking about spooky things can turn off some people and you will find doors slamming in your face and phone lines clicking as people hang up. I recommend stating that you are doing research on the land in question and if the person knew anything about the previous owners that might not be well-known. I find that the older generation is a wealth of information on not only neighbors, but also on the town. They will remember what stood on the street corner before the shopping mall was built. They will remember who was dating who, and who was cheating on who. They may even remember who was ranting that there was a ghost in their home. There are several ways to gently approach the topic of what was happening before the client moved in. If you can effectively gather this information without announcing it to the world that Mr. Smith believes there's a ghost in his bathroom, then you will be well on your way to figuring out what is going on.

I have found that in the cases of military neighborhoods, since the government seals records on residency, talking to locals will be a good start. While the neighbors will be moving in and out every few years, they also have built a tight-knit community where everyone looks out for each other, especially when a deployment is concerned. Sometimes the client will offer to have their neighbors come over and talk with you, or even participate in the house blessing or cleansing. Again, use your best judgment on approaching this. You want to leave the client's reputation intact by the time this is over, regardless of having permission from the client. In the event that you don't have permission from the client to speak to their neighbors, you can still make calls to the local historians. I recommend against speaking to neighbors in close proximity of the client, as they will most likely see you entering the client's residence. If the interviewee directly asks whether or not the client is experiencing paranormal activity, ask them why they would ask such a question, and you'll probably get the information that you're looking for while still maintaining the client's privacy.

It's a tough line to walk when trying to maintain confidentiality, making sure the doors don't close on you, and conducting in-depth research. In all honesty, practice makes perfect. The more you interview and talk to different people, the more you will be able to use your best judgment and gauge how far to go when seeking testimonies of people outside of the client.

Similar Cases

Another department of historical research is searching through case files of your team, organizations, and journals such as the Society for Psychical Research and the Rhine Research Center to see if they have ever dealt with a similar case such as yours. Parapsychology is a world of networking and sharing information, and it is possible that there was a similar occurrence out there in the past century. If this is the case, then you will have a solid foundation in communication with the presence and implementing a solution from those who were successful. This is one of the reasons why APS maintains case records. There are other teams who will also make their previous cases available online, or solo investigators who have written books or articles on their most compelling cases. If you find yourself in the midst of a case where you are stuck, doing this extra legwork would be most beneficial. While it's not historical research that is directly related to your case, it is a link that can help with your problem-solving.

Records, Records, Records

In my experience of conducting historical research, I have found that witness testimony can be shaky and like a game of telephone. Meaning that the stories that have been passed down throughout the generations may be completely inaccurate. While this may be disheartening, it's to be expected. It doesn't mean that the drama or hope is lost when conducting historical research.

In order to ensure that your historical research is accurate, you will have to obtain basic knowledge of record keeping. One of the earliest forms of record keeping is the United States Census, which is taken every ten years, starting in 1790. There, you will obtain information on households including parents, children, race, ages, and income. Believe it or not, birth certificates, death certificates and marriage licenses did not start at the same time in the United States. Instead, states started to maintain them sporadically. For example, New York State started issuing birth certificates just before the Civil War. Numerous immigrants that came to the United States didn't have any records on them at all. In the mid-1800's more states started to jump on board with birth certificates.

If you run into a brick wall in terms of certificates of birth or death, all hope is not lost. This means you must go to the church. If you look into church records, you will find baptismal certificates, which can go back as far as the 1500's. Family Bibles also tend to have records of birth and deaths of family members. Just as important, you need to learn the jargon and language of the era that you're researching. Terminology has changed dramatically in the last one hundred years, and the last thing you want to do is misinterpret your data due to a lack of knowledge of terminology of the time. Make friends with the state and national archives, and if a word sounds odd, do some digging and see if the historical context might have changed the word, giving it a different meaning.

As you can see, there are numerous avenues you can take when you're conducting historical research. It is crucial that you do this for your investigations. Will you be able to go into as much detail with each case? No, but try to make the best effort to do so. Not only will this help you when it comes to communicating with the presence, but it also give you and your team valuable information when you're about to close a case. Neglecting to conduct any research is like going into battle without your armor. There could be a ghost just waiting for the right context to be presented to them so they can communicate. You want to make sure that you're armed with the knowledge needed to ask the right questions.

CHAPTER 8
CLOSING A CASE

After you have conducted your investigation, you're more than halfway there towards closing the case. I will be honest and say that APS doesn't close a case immediately. We will keep our cases open for a significant period of time, which will vary depending on the nature of the case. This is where your client will figure out, once and for all, whether you were the best choice in handling their needs. Closing a case is much more than packing up your equipment and saying that you're all finished.

I want to emphasize that if this case regards dealing with a haunting for years, you won't be able to resolve it in less than a week. I've noticed that a lot of teams want to emphasize speed, walk in with their "proton packs" so to speak, do their thing, and leave. Paranormal reality shows have also made it appear as though investigators can walk in and take care of business in a matter of days. Then, when teams are taking weeks, or even months to deal with a case, they think it is a reflection of their skills.

In your team's lifetime, you will deal with a variety of cases that will need a variety of resolutions. From clients who are okay with their ghost to the family that wanted everything out yesterday, there won't be two cases that are exactly the same. Luckily, each case you work on will prepare you for the next case. You will be more knowledgeable and more confident with each investigation, and you will also see the growth in your team members.

When it comes to closing out a case, there are different areas that you will touch on with your client.

Evidence Review & Presentation

After the investigation is over, the team will go through the audio and video evidence that they captured from each night. This means that you'll have many hours of evidence to go through. This may not seem like much help, but the more you go through evidence, the better you'll get at detecting anomalies through scanning the frames, shots, waveforms, etc. The area for me that can be hard to short cut through is audio. But in my experience, I've found that anomalies will normally have an abnormal pattern, such as a spike, a section that may be curvy (as opposed to straight lines), basically something that will not match the rest of the waveforms.

There are numerous audio programs you can use for review. The best one that numerous investigators have used is Audacity. Not only is it great for evidence review, but it is also free. I also use free audio editing programs on my computer if I'm in a pinch, but I find that it can compress files and compromise your audio quality. As you get used to different programs, continue to experiment with them and see what works best for you.

Having more than one set of eyes is also crucial for evidence review. If the load is too much, we will ask the California team to assist. If anything, their input might be more valuable because they haven't looked at the property before. When it comes to reviewing audio as well, we will not tell each other what we heard until we have confirmed everyone is done with their evidence review, and we will come together and discuss as a group with our thoughts already prepared.

There is one more way to help save time on evidence review, and that is to keep track of what is going on in and throughout the investigation, and if something happens, what time it occurred. This will require that you cue your recorders together by making some sort of noise that will carry, which will usually be clapping. If someone is having an experience or feeling off, record what time it happened so that you can go directly to that time stamp. Same thing goes for video and photography. Finally, taking an introductory course in tech, as mentioned earlier, will help throw out evidence that can be attributed to moisture, dust, device function, etc.

When presenting the evidence to your client, it is another way of confirming and validating their experience. Your experience in their home or business is valuable, but there is something special about evidence review. It is their chance to see their fears, questions, and curiosities validated. I don't show the client hundreds of hours of evidence, but instead, prepare clips with a brief summary of what time the data was collected and what was going on during this time, if applicable.

There are a variety of ways you can do the evidence review. It is more personable to arrive with your computer, flat screen, and headphones. It also gives you the opportunity to see the client's reactions in real time and be readily available to answer questions. As I said earlier, I will not tell the client what to hear when it comes to audio, I will play the clip and ask them what they thought they heard and share what the team thought. You don't want to influence the client and make them fearful of something that is not there.

The other option, especially if working on a long distance case, is to set up an online venue where the client can review the evidence at home. The client's reactions are more private, but it also gives them the evidence to download and keep. This can be a bit controversial, depending on the nature of the case. I've found that there is an even mix between clients who want to keep their evidence (which might end up being the star at their next party), and others who don't want any sort of lasting memory of the haunting.

This is where you might have to step in and be firm. If the haunting is a negative influence and the client wants to keep the souvenir, you will need to inform the client how hanging on to the evidence may be counter-productive and even invite the presence back. This is a "buyer beware" area, because the client may still want to keep the evidence after the warning. With APS, we do not withhold evidence from the client regardless because it was recorded on the client's property with their permission. We can advise and recommend until our faces turn blue, but it is still the client's call.

Finally, we do not post evidence on our website from our client investigations. Even if we think that we have the Holy Grail when it comes to proving ghosts exist. Oftentimes, I will send evidence to one or two colleagues to get their input on what may have caused the anomaly, and I'll get some new insight. This may seem a bit pessimistic, but even if I post evidence that is without a doubt proof that ghosts are real, not everyone will believe it. Posting evidence has proven to have too many unanswered questions and variables that lead to discussions that turn into arguments. Even if you're not involved in the conversation, people will argue amongst themselves. For APS, it isn't worth the drama. We use our evidence as learning tools for ourselves, and perhaps the one or two outside sources (who have also signed confidentiality agreements) that we bring in for a second opinion. If you are a team that posts your client's evidence online, all I say to that is make sure you have the client's permission, even if you don't mention their names or the nature of the case. You never know who has walked into that house, and then runs into your website.

Diagnosis & Solution

Here we come to the meat and potatoes of APS investigations. Since we are a solutions-based team, we do a lot of research and networking to ensure that the phenomenon is taken care of. This could mean clearing the house, or mediating between the dead and the living. We've run into numerous cases where the client misunderstood the presence, and once an understanding was reached, the home dynamic improved tremendously.

In order to properly solve a case, we have to figure out what exactly is going on. For example, I wouldn't advise doing an exorcism for the presence of an old lady's ghost who is just hanging around and not interacting with the clients. However, if the client wants the activity to stop, this will normally mean that whatever is present needs to go away. This means that identifying exactly what is in the space is crucial because there isn't one clean-cut way to clear the space of a haunting. There are numerous variables that impact the way a solution could work.

A good place to begin is to find out what religion the client believes in, if any. Most of our clients are Christian, which usually means praying and blessing the property. The reason why we want to stay within the realm of the client's religion is because there is power in faith, whether or not you agree with it. There is immense power in "will and intent" and in the mind and soul. If the client believes the solution will work, their belief will add power into the solution as its being implemented. You will also expand your knowledge in different religions as well, so it is a win-win situation. If the client has no religious affiliation, then you have to determine the client's comfort level in implementing religious solutions. If they aren't comfortable with blessings, then perhaps mental visualizations will be effective.

With any religious-centric solution, you want to be honest with yourself with how much spiritual authority you have personally. This is where you might find yourself contacting the client's religious leader, or local clergy around the area to see if they can oversee and implement a blessing or cleansing. You don't want to do this yourself, as the client will not only respect the religious leader, but the spiritual world will as well. You don't want to be the 5-year old walking around in Dad's shoes that are too big for you.

Also, I like to add an extra touch with stones and bury them on the four corners of the property. The type of stones I'll include is rose quartz, black tourmaline, hematite, and citrine. Rose quartz attracts love, black tourmaline deflects the negative energy and puts it into the ground, hematite shields and protects, and citrine clears negativity and attracts positive energy for happiness. This is a basic recipe, it doesn't mean you need to do it. If you want to utilize stones, talk to your client and see what their thoughts are. The utilization of crystals dates back to the ancient Sumerian in the form of magic formulas as well as for jewelry. The evolution and history to using stones and crystals is well worth researching.

If your client is okay with the activity, and just wanted to identify who is in the space, then your job is nearly done. It doesn't mean pack up and go home. You can talk with your client about setting boundaries, shielding techniques, and leave your contact information for them to call you should they need more advice.

You don't want to pressure your client to do anything they don't want to do in regards to the solution. The team has the pleasure to pack up and go home, the client stays there. You will implement many different types of solutions in your team's lifetime, and being there to support your client is one of the most important things you can do.

Client Dynamics & Responsibility

So far, with every case I have worked on, I have found that the client's dynamic will have an impact on the haunting. Once you have figured out what is going on in the residence or business, you need to factor in the client's involvement in the activity. This doesn't mean that the client was escalating the haunting on purpose. This could mean that the overprotective ghost became more active after the head of the household left home on business, or the client has been contemplating suicide and their deceased loved ones were trying to intervene and communicate. I have found that the hauntings are a response to the client and/or an attempt to communicate with the client. There is a specific reason why they are there, and if the "unfinished business" so to speak is reasonable and for the benefit of the client's life, then APS will mediate some sort of communication between the two parties. This is also the reason why APS will keep the client on the property while we investigate. This situation is much similar to solving a case of miscommunication between loved ones.

Teach a Man to Fish

One of the philosophies of APS is to teach our clients and empower them with information. We don't do this as a way to dodge any follow up visits, but instead to give the clients a way to handle their situation and any future hauntings on their own. They are still always welcome to call us at any time. We will have print outs of basic paranormal information such as terminology, shielding and grounding techniques, along with history of paranormal investigating, and how to look at their pictures and debunk things such as orbs, focus issues and light streaks. This education aspect doesn't have to wait until the investigation is over. In fact, it can start as soon as you walk through the client's door. I find that if the client is showing us photos of what they perceive as the ghost, and I am seeing photos of dust, I will be honest with the client and explain to them what they are seeing in the photo.

When to Walk Away

Unfortunately, there will be times when you close a case because you had to walk away. In our experience, APS will walk away from a case when the client isn't taking responsibility for their actions, there is an overwhelming amount of evidence for mental illness, there is the influence of drugs present, or not doing what they need to be doing to resolve their case such as not engaging with the presence, unburying stones, playing with a Ouija board, asking the presence to come back, etc. It is always a difficult decision to do this, but you have to keep your and your team's best interest at heart in terms of time, dedication, and safety. It isn't worth jeopardizing your own mental peace by stressing yourself out with a client that doesn't trust you, listen to you, or follow your advice or suggestions.

It can be initially perceived that walking away from a case is giving up or a negative experience, but it doesn't always have to be. This kind of peace comes with the acceptance that while you can't control the actions of others, you can control your own emotions and responses. Being completely honest on your views, and speaking out of compassion and love will usually have a calm response from the client. If the situation turns negative, walk away, and don't look back. If you're walking away because you feel the client has a medical issue, be careful while treading the line between telling the client to seek medical attention and diagnosing them with a health problem (and citing it as the reason you're walking away).

We have often dealt with clients who were told by another team that they have a brain tumor or they are schizophrenic. We find that it is a different situation. It's a fine line. There was only once that the team in Raleigh has had to walk away from a case where the client was previously diagnosed with schizophrenia and was having hallucinations from their medication. This information was disclosed to us. In this event, we spoke to the client's daughter (who didn't believe there was anything paranormal happening in the first place), and we told her that we felt our presence would be more harmful than beneficial for the client in their treatment. But if the client's doctor disagreed with us, then we have them send us a signed letter. We never heard from this client again, and I truly hope they received the help they needed.

But we have found that some clients just enjoy the attention, or they want to be able to tell their friends that they got a bunch of ghost hunters in their house. In this situation, you will be stuck in a whirlwind of circles that will not end unless you walk away, or the client turns on you. At APS, we try to not leave the client empty-handed in the event that we have to walk away. We will usually recommend another team or an individual who can better assist. Use your best judgment and follow your instincts should the topic of walking away ever occur.

Follow Up

After you close a case, while you may want to follow up immediately, the next day even, you will want to give them some space to settle into their adjusted life. No matter what, paranormal experiences can change a person and it could even rock their world a bit. It could be the disillusioned husband whose wife got validation that there was a ghost in the house, or a child learning that their imaginary friend was the kid who drowned in the lake fifty years earlier.

I tend to wait about three days before my first follow up call. I will talk to the client and ask them the following questions:

- How has it been since we left?
- Are you noticing any changes in the environment?
- Are you still having experiences? Have they increased or decreased since we were there?
- Is there anything that seems weird to you right now?
- How has your family adjusted?
- Is everyone sleeping through the night?
- Does everyone feel safe at home?
- Are you comfortable being home alone?
- Do you have any questions for me?

Depending on the answers to these questions, after the three day follow up, I'll then move on to a weekly follow up. First I'll start with a phone call, and then I'll ask the client if they want to continue the follow up via email. This way, you're respecting not only the client's time, but your time as well if the aftermath of the investigation is positive. If there is still residual activity, depending on the severity of the activity and how the client feels about it, you may have to make a follow up visit just to check in.

Media

Sometimes APS will receive mass emails from television producers looking for stories for their next season. While we don't pursue television opportunities ourselves, I will pass the information on to our clients since they might have interest. Never do we put pressure on a client to go to the media with their story. Anything that they do, we usually request to be left out of it, unless we are asked to be interviewed. The primary goal of the team is case resolution, not to seek our 15-minutes of fame. I have met teams that have aggressively put pressure on their clients to go to the news and seek out guest spots on television shows so that they will be called in to give their testimony. I feel that they have the team's interest in fame as their top priority and not the client's situation.

Going forward to the media is really a personal decision for the client to make on their own without pressure. Their face and name will be publicly associated with the paranormal and ghosts. We are still living in an age where this isn't widely accepted. While there have been advances in the acceptance of the paranormal thanks to the media, there are still negative connotations. It can potentially affect the client's employment, their children's social interactions, and dynamics with friends and family. I feel preserving personal lives is more important than any sort of media exposure for my team, but again.

If our clients choose to seek media attention, and they get it, I sincerely hope that by them sharing their story, they will be able to help others. If they choose to involve my team in the proceedings, then I consider it an honor. Media attention tends to be decent PR for your team, and you'll probably receive an influx of case submissions after publication or airing of your client's story. The media has to come to us. We don't push it on the clients, but instead slide the information under the door.

When Is a Case Officially Closed?

At APS, we don't close cases right away. Instead, we will keep the case open for about 6 months, as the follow ups reduce. I go with the idea that "no news is good news", meaning that things are quiet and calm. We still want to respect the client's privacy and personal space, and phasing ourselves out is a matter of respect and moving on. This is a short answer to the heading, but we will close the case based on the client's satisfaction or silence.

Sometimes closing a case doesn't necessarily mean that it's solved, it means that the client is no longer in need of our services anymore. In a perfect world, we would be able to solve every case that comes out way and life would be grand. But sometimes, whether it's a personality clash, dynamic, or butting heads, it's just not meant to be to work with this specific client. And that is okay!

I give the team about a month to complete their case reports before turning them in for our records. This way, if the case reopens, or we find ourselves in a similar case in the future, we can pull up those records. The better you keep your data, the easier it will be to go back and grab it in the times you need it, regardless of the context.

CHAPTER 9
MOVING FORWARD

One of the most important things that you and your team can do to continue to move forward is engage in ongoing research. There is more out there than just residential cases. There are different theories and methodologies to explore. You want to be as educated and informed as you can be not just for your residential cases, but also for your own research.

I require that my team members constantly be doing some sort of independent research. I tend to stay in the area of theory and integrating my theatre training into investigating, while other team members may research different types of tech, techniques in historical research, and more. We are a group that strives to study and learn more about the paranormal on a regular basis. We join groups on social media, engage in discussion about theories with other investigators around the world. With the innovation of social media, we can connect with so many people today.

We have even become donors for organizations such as the Rhine Research Center and the Society for Psychical Research. Reading periodicals will keep you and your team updated in what is going on in parapsychological research. There is also The Ghost Club in the United Kingdom and countless other groups that are using the scientific method to analyze not only the human brain's relationship with their external environment (psychics, clairvoyance, astral projection, remote viewing, etc.), but some that are also diving into afterlife research and whether or not ghosts exists. Dr. Piero Calvi-Parisetti wrote a book called *21 Days into the Afterlife*, which documents his theories and thoughts about the survival of consciousness after death. He is a doctor who is now a bereavement counselor, so he has the education to back up his theories. There is fascinating research out there besides going on regular ghost hunts.

I strongly emphasize looking into the academic side of the paranormal, rather than putting heavy focus on the entertainment side such as television shows, online videos, slideshows, etc. that offer little-to-no explanation or back story. I also say beware of those who only expect you to accept their opinion, and discourage questions to verify, or even challenge their thoughts. One of the most exciting parts of this field to me is that no one really has the exact same theory or definition for things. This leaves room to have productive debates about these subjects, but not many in the paranormal field want to engage in it. If you run into someone who is willing to go into an academic-like banter with you, and you can still walk away as friends, keep them close! This field wouldn't be interesting at all if we all just agreed with each other all the time.

When you encourage your team to conduct research, don't force them to research something they might not be interested in (of course, unless it is for a case). Otherwise, your members probably won't do the research as well as they should, if they do it at all. When I train new members for APS, they go through trainings for different theories and methodologies, plus quizzes and research papers. The prompts for the papers are intentionally vague because I want to train knowledgeable investigators and critical thinkers as well. You don't want a team full of sheep who will accept anything you say at point blank. You want them to agree with you, but for the right reasons. After analyzing the evidence and data, the team needs to be able to think critically and come up with their own conclusions. It's really a beautiful set up.

Thinking critically can sometimes have a negative connotation. But in truth, it's an exploration towards acceptance or rejection of an idea. Critical thinkers will often take notes in books, having a conversation with the author. They will ask questions, listen, and then ask follow up questions. They can sometimes be perceived as annoying or as a group of troublemakers, but they want to not just learn, but understand why. Sometimes they may even know their answers already, but will ask someone for their interpretation of an answer. Critical thinkers keep us on our toes, and most importantly, keep us thinking and exploring. I consider it flattering when I engage in a debate with a critical thinker, even if it does make me nervous.

Speaking of being nervous, I can only speak for myself when it comes to being nervous and hesitant in engaging in conversation with others outside of my team. Usually, it is because I am afraid of being wrong. Since taking on a more active role in the field, I have had to learn that it is absolutely okay to be wrong! This is a concept that I personally feel many miss in the paranormal field, which is one of the reasons why there are so many hurt feelings, fights, and slander in the field. It seems that there are those that feel in order to "save face" so to speak, they have to go on to publicly slam another person after a debate or fight.

In moving forward, also consider other methodologies of investigating. One of my favorites is the "E4" method by Brian D. Parsons, the executive director of the group ParaNexus. This man knows his stuff and his approaches to client-centered cases are both traditional and non-traditional through his knowledge of parapsychology, interviewing specialists, and integrating different methodologies. I had the pleasure of meeting Brian at the 2nd annual "Ghost Excavation Conference" in 2013, headed by John G. Sabol. I found that his method makes a lot of sense and is practical in the work of residential cases from beginning to end.

Speaking of Mr. Sabol, he is the man behind the "Ghost Excavation" methodology, which integrates performance and archaeological techniques into communication with the dead. Essentially, it means to bring the context of the dead to them, rather than forcing them to conform to our modern day world. For example, using lingo and terminology from the 21st century would not be effective in trying to communicate with a deceased Union soldier on a Civil War battlefield. What Mr. Sabol does is dress in period clothing and brings in scenes or scenarios to the space, and then sees what responds or becomes unearthed. It is so different from mainstream paranormal investigating, but it is effective, as I have seen it firsthand. Mr. Sabol has written countless books about the "ghost excavation" method, along with his ongoing research of haunted locations. I have found this method produces extraordinary results because the spirits identify something and someone familiar to them, and they respond. The evidence that Mr. Sabol and his partner, Mary Becker, have collected is nothing short of mind-boggling.

This is a beautiful example of methodologies going hand-in-hand. When you see this occurring, it is worth taking a look. Another researcher to take into consideration for your studies is Robin Bellamy. She is not only a genealogist, but she is very knowledgeable in the forensic field along with the paranormal field with experience in working on residential cases as well as other areas of the paranormal realm, especially cryptozoology. If you need assistance in gathering information on deeds and property information, she is your gal. Ms. Bellamy is a wealth of knowledge who is also available to assist and answer questions.

The three individuals I just mentioned are a great resource of information. Networking in the community is so important, and researching is a great way to start in figuring out who would be a good person to network with. There's a saying that goes like, "You never want to be the smartest person in the room." It's very true. You want to be continuously learning from others. It will help you grow as a researcher and investigator, making you a very valuable person when it comes to working with clients and in society in general.

Another part of moving forward is accepting that you do not know everything. I highly recommend taking online courses from reputable groups such as the Rhine Research Center and the HCH Institute. One of HCH's most well-known teacher is none other than Loyd Auerbach. He is the director of the Office of Paranormal Investigations as well as serving on the board of directors for the Rhine. Mr. Auerbach has written numerous books on paranormal subjects and is a highly sought after expert in the field. Along with his courses, he also offers mentoring services. He does charge for his time, but I have no issue with it as he has the credentials, knowledge, and reputation to support it. I can't recommend him enough to paranormal investigators who want to not only learn more, but learn how to help clients with their paranormal problems. He holds an MS in Parapsychology from JFK University, which he obtained in 1981 when parapsychology was a more expanded study in universities.

Never. Stop. Learning. If you, or a team member, feels that "expert level" has been reached to the point where you think you have nothing else to learn, look again.

Also, while I feel that clients should not be charged to have a group come investigate, I don't see an issue with credentialed experts charging for their books and classes. While there are no longer degrees in the paranormal, there are educated people in this field who have earned bachelors, masters, and doctorate degrees in their field of study. Pay attention to these people! They are a wealth of information and new ideas, and considering that they are dedicating their time to educate others, I am more than happy to grab some cash and buy their books. An expert is not someone who has been on television. And in reality, some of the experts that are "lesser known" have been used as consultants on the television shows that the public know and love. Be sure to check the background of any person or organization that offers classes or mentoring for a price. If you believe you would get your money's worth, then by all means, sign up.

The final thing that you and your team should consider is attending events. I don't mean just the large paranormal conventions featuring people who have been on television or radio, but the academic-type gatherings as well. Sometimes you will learn a tremendous amount of information from these sessions, and sometimes you won't. However, you will not know unless you attend. If you're making a decision of whether to attend or not, do a search online on the guest names and check out what they're currently doing in the paranormal field. If it is of interest to you, then buy the ticket to the event.

Moving forward means keeping things fresh for your team. Whether it is new knowledge, a concept you want to discuss, or interacting with the paranormal community, moving forward means progressing in your passion.

CONCLUSION

We have reached the end of our journey. It is my sincere hope that this book was enlightening and a good read for you. I hope that you got a lot out of the book, or even learned from my mistakes as I was getting the Association of Paranormal Study off the ground. It is my hope that APS lasts for the next several decades and even survives without me after I depart or pass on.

I am very interested in watching the paranormal field over the next few years. The paranormal reality shows aren't as plentiful at the present moment, and the "draw" or the fan base is changing since the television aspect is moving in a different direction. If we want the paranormal community to be taken seriously, we need to start paying attention when someone has something to say in terms of rebuking claims, thoughts, and theories. As the people on the receiving end of the disagreement, you have extraordinary power to change the dynamic of the conversation from a fight to a productive discussion; knowing when to ignore a troll and walk away. I would love to see the paranormal community become a thriving area that will help the fringe sciences embark on a path to where they are heavily considered in the academic and scientific field. The paranormal community is being watched, and we need to consider our own words and behavior and how it represents the field.

If you're reading this book as someone who is hoping to start their own team in the future, you're off to a great start. It's not because you're reading this particular book specifically, but the fact that you are reading a book in the first place. It may seem trivial, but there are groups out there who have only watched the television shows and decided that they wanted to become ghost hunters. Reading books will give you information and insight on the works of others, and you can also see the growth of the paranormal field over the course of its existence. Read about how the perception of death has changed over the last few centuries. Read how society's perceptions of ghosts have evolved and how humanity expressed their belief in the afterlife. Read scientific journals, even if you don't understand them at first. With patience, practice, and utilizing the Internet, you can read about the innovations and developments in the scientific community. Being a good paranormal researcher and investigator means that you are constantly learning about yourself and the world around you.

If you're a member of a team, keep reading as well. Be a beacon of knowledge and hope for your team. Regardless of whether you want to rise up into a leadership position, you are still a valuable team member who can bring a lot to the table. You have the power to help lessen stress by spending an extra few minutes helping your director set up and break down equipment. You have the power to support a team member who may be feeling fearful or that the case is way over their head. You have the power to add a bit of hope and light to a client's day when the activity escalates in their home to the point where they're not sure they can handle it anymore.

Ultimately, while there are numerous experts and scholars in the paranormal field, we must not forget that there are people out there who are completely new to this world. Many are feeling alienated and alone, and yearn to have someone to talk to them who doesn't think they are crazy, and perhaps could even add some clarity to their life. As investigators, we have the opportunity to change lives for the better and train up the future researchers of the field.

If there is one last bit of advice I can offer, it is to be kind to one another. Whether you believe in reincarnation, a heaven, hell, etc. being kind will lessen the drama in your life along with making others around you feel accepted. So far, we can only prove that we only live this particular life once, so let us make the most of it! As I mentioned before, your good name in this field is everything. What will people think when they hear your name? Strive for better, and strive for peace with the goal of fostering productive conversations.

I wish you the best in this field. Be kind, be strong, keep learning, ask questions, believe everything, be skeptical, train harder, and persevere.

RECOMMENDED READING

Below are books I recommend to get you started in not only ghost hunting, but taking on residential cases in the investigation field. They are written by people who have established themselves in the field as professionals who have tested their methods on the field with success. Even if you are experienced in the field, the following books are a great read.

Books by Loyd Auerbach
A Paranormal Casebook: Ghost Hunting in the Millennium
Ghost Hunting: How to Investigate the Paranormal
Hauntings and Poltergeists: A Ghost Hunter's Guide

Books by Brian D. Parsons
The "E4" Method
Handbook for the Amateur Paranormal Investigator or Ghost Hunter
Handbook for the Amateur Paranormal Investigator or Ghost Hunter: Part II
Betty's Ghost: A Guide to Paranormal Investigation

Books by John G. Sabol
Digging Up Ghosts: Unearthing Past Presences at a Haunted Location
Ghost Culture: Theories, Context and Scientific Practices
The Ghost Excavation

ABOUT THE AUTHOR

Alex Matsuo is the founder and director of the group, Association of Paranormal Study (APS), which started in 2011. Before that, she was an independent paranormal investigator who worked with different teams in Southern California as well as conducting historical research and case management. She is the author of the books, *The Haunted Actor*, *10,000 Words*, and *The Haunting of the Tenth Avenue Theater*, which is based on her memoirs of acting and working in a haunted theatre in San Diego, CA, published by Llewellyn. When she is not working on paranormal-related activities, Alex an actor, dramaturg, and playwright. She is also a paranormal radio host and podcaster, currently hosting the show, "The Wicked Domain" on LiveParanormal.com and History.FM.

Alex received her Master of Arts in theatre arts from San Diego State University in 2011 and currently resides in Raleigh, North Carolina working as a teacher and podcaster. You can find more information about Alex at www.alexmatsuo.com and APS at www.associationofparanormalstudy.com.

Made in the USA
Middletown, DE
18 May 2015